Creative Designs with Children at Worship

A. Roger Gobbel and Phillip C. Huber

John Knox Press
ATLANTA

Library of Congress Cataloging in Publication Data

Gobbel, A   Roger, 1926-
  Creative designs with children at worship.

  Bibliography: p.
  1.Children's liturgies. 2. Children—Religious
life. I. Huber, Phillip C., joint author. II. Title.
BV199.C4G6   264   80-82225
ISBN 0-8042-1526-X (pbk.)

©copyright John Knox Press 1981
10 9 8 7 6 5 4 3 2 1
Printed in the United States of America
John Knox Press
Atlanta, Georgia 30365

Preface

This book has emerged from a long struggle with the question, "What is the place and role of children in the gathered, worshiping community?" It is offered as one response, certainly not as a final answer, to that question. We have designed the book for parish pastors who desire to engage children along with all in the worship of the gathered congregation.

We begin with a brief theological statement asserting that the proper and rightful place of Christian children is in the gathered, worshiping community, sharing and doing the worship of congregation. That statement shifts attention and concern from "What can we do *for* children during worship?" to "What can we do *along with* children in worship so that all of us together may do the proper work of the community?"

A series of strategies organized around the Christian church year and intended to be implemented during worship services composes the larger portion of this work. The strategies, informed by the theological statement noted above, are cognizant of both the abilities and limitations of children and will assist the children in doing worship as they are able. The strategy descriptions are rooted in actual practice, reflecting the experiences of the authors in congregational settings.

We are indebted to many persons who have made significant contributions to the development of this book: to friends and colleagues who made suggestions for strategy content; to the congregation of St. John's Lutheran Church, Harpers Ferry, West Virginia, the setting of the initial testing of strategies; to Connie Huber who critiqued the initial implementations of strategies; to Donald N. Matthews, librarian at the Lutheran Theological Seminary at Gettysburg, who made suggestions for reworking parts of the manuscript; to Gertrude G. Gobbel, associate professor of psychology, Gettysburg College, who gave invaluable assistance related to language, content, and sequencing of materials in the strategy descriptions; and to Mary C. Miller who, with haste and excellence, typed the several stages of the manuscript. To them we express our gratitude. Obviously, any errors or shortcomings belong to us and not to them.

A.R.G.
P.C.H.

Contents

For Josh and Bekky

I. Children in the Gathered, Worshiping Community

I. Children in the Gathered, Worshiping Community

Children complain, "Church? It's boring." Parents observe, "There is nothing in the worship service for children." And clergy ask, "What can we do for children in worship?" Out of particular concerns and feelings each group identifies anew a long-time, bothersome problem for the church. What is the place and role of children in the gathered, worshiping community? We have sought diligently to discover adequate and satisfying responses. Our search has frequently ended in frustration, and we have been tempted to abandon it. In our temptation we experience uneasiness and concern which serve to compel us in a continuing search. The problem identified by children, parents, and clergy has pushed hard upon us, and its solution has eluded us.

Many factors contribute to our dilemma. Let us consider here just one which is of powerful consequence. As in the past even now, worship is regarded primarily as the work of the adult congregation. This view suggests that the celebrations of the community have very little to do with children. So long as it is the dominant view, whatever is done with children in worship will remain tangential to the work of the gathered community. Our efforts will be little more than "tinkering around," achieving more frustration and disappointment.

Worship regarded primarily as an adult activity encourages the exclusion of children from the gathered, worshiping community by either geography or concern. Though intended not at all, the exclusion is very common in Christian congregations. We recognize it; we are disturbed by it. With some regularity we struggle with the question, "What can we do *for* our children during the worship service?" Children's (junior) church, children's choirs, church school during the worship service, nurseries for preschoolers, and children's sermons, sometimes with object lessons—these have been our most favorite programmatic responses. The popularity of each rises and falls. Few of us are pleased with the results. It is highly probable that we have been asking the wrong question: What can we do *for* our children in worship? Guided by wrong or inappropriate questions concerning a problem, we inevitably arrive at wrong or inadequate solutions.

3

In recent years a new interest in children and worship has emerged. Books of children's sermons and liturgies are in abundance. Many clergy individually are struggling with the problem. The new interest, rooted not only in a concern for children but also prompted by new directions in theology and liturgy, occasions fresh opportunities for us to explore and propose more compelling and satisfying responses to the larger question: What is the place and role of children in the gathered, worshiping community? This book is offered as one effort in that exploration and proposal.

Children Belong in the Gathered, Worshiping Community

When the Christian community gathers for worship, all of its members should be encouraged to participate. Worship is the celebration of all the community's people of all ages together. Our children belong to that community. In the gathered congregation we dare not expect our children to sit as passive spectators. Rather, we welcome them as members of the household of faith, encouraging their active involvement in the life and work of the household. Something significant is tragically lost not only for the children but for all of us when they, either by design or default, are excluded from active sharing in the community's celebrations.

A particular theological bias informs this book. Courtesy and honesty demand a clear and simple statement of that bias which has implications not only for children in the worshiping congregation but for the whole of Christian education. It is the bias of infant baptism. By virtue of their baptism our children belong to the Christian church. So the problem is not, Where should our children be? The answer is clear: our children's rightful and proper place is with and in the gathered, worshiping community. More than that, they, along with all the people of all ages, are to share in doing the congregation's worship.

In the gathered community are those words, stories, symbols, cultic acts and events which identify all of us together as Christian. How the children may understand those identifications intellectually and affectively is not our first concern at this point. Rather, children in the gathered, worshiping community are totally surrounded by those identifications which proclaim to them the reality of who they already are, while continuing to point to that reality in ever new, exciting ways. That is a matter of first concern. So, whatever we do with children vis-à-vis worship or in the activity of Christian education, our task in the first instance is not that of "making" Christians of them. We are charged however, with the work of socialization within the Christian community, of ongoing conversion, and of assisting children to claim their baptism. Our task is to help our children to be and do who they already are, and to learn what it is to be Christian together.

To a very large extent we have been tyrannized by the improper question, What can we do *for* our children during worship? Again, our most frequent responses have been the junior church, worship in the church school, and children's sermons. Regardless of how popular these approaches have been, they suffer from a number of inadequacies. With one exception, the concern here is not to identify and discuss those inadequacies. Those most frequent responses tend to isolate and exclude children from the total worship life of the congregation. They are often regarded as "nice" things to do *for* the children. They become isolated events *for* the children or "operations" performed on the children by adults. All too often they prevent the children's interaction and engagement with the total life of the gathered community. Even the junior sermon tends to isolate children within a group of peers. Somewhat aside, many of us are distressed when adults tell us that they "get more out of" the children's sermon than the "regular" sermon. Such comments present us with a temptation to which we must not succumb. We should never misuse the children's sermon or anything else we do with children in worship by making adults the primary target audience of our efforts. Such would be a dreadful misuse of the children themselves.

The question, What can we do *for* our children during worship? is not only improper but is misleading. The more fruitful and exciting, yet more difficult and demanding, question is, What shall we do *along with* children so that all of us together may do the proper work of the community? In responding to this question we take seriously who our children already are, affirm their already given place in the community, and declare that they do belong. We point them to the reality given by our Lord—his church.

Given opportunities within their abilities, our children can share and participate actively in the celebrations of the gathered, worshiping community. Not as adults nor even as adolescents but as children they can take their place along with all others in doing worship. They can give praise; they can make an offering; they can say prayers; they can speak a word from God. Their doing worship will enrich the community's total celebrations and may occasionally serve as a model for adults in doing worship. Indeed, the children may lead them. In whatever we do *along with* children in worship, our task is to enable Christian children, indeed the whole congregation, in the constant discovery of who they already are, to challenge them to become and do who they are and to encourage them in doing the community's worship. From their life in the gathered, worshiping community our children may discover and come to know in ever expanding dimensions the reality into which they have been baptized.

Participation Is Learning

Increasingly we are entertaining the possibility that the gathered, worshiping community may well be the church's most potent and influential educational arm. If we take a long look, we should not be surprised that the impact and contributions of the gathered community for Christian nurture and growth may well far exceed those of formal church schooling. These comments are not to be interpreted as an attack upon, for example, the Sunday church school. Rather, they are intended to give clear focus to the pervasive, powerful educational dimension of worship.

Some will argue that worship is not Christian education and that the two should never be coupled in any fashion, not even in conversation. They fear that by linkage of the two, Christian worship will be downgraded, eroded, or even negated. The concern is to be regarded seriously and not dismissed lightly. But regardless of the arguments presented for a sharp separation of the two a clear, undeniable fact remains. There is an educational dimension in the doing of worship. We learn to be the church as we experience the church; we learn to worship in doing worship; we learn to be the worshiping community as we do the work of the community; we learn to be and do Christian as we do worship. The "purists" may insist doggedly upon their distinctions but they do so to the detriment of the Christian community.

In our life as Christians there is always the dynamic of "being" and "becoming," the dynamic of learning to become what we already are.

And so it is with our children. The most appropriate, nourishing environment in which that "being" and "becoming" is realized is not worship in the church school, not the junior church, not even formal church schooling, as useful and as important as they may be. It is the gathered, worshiping community. Here the whole congregation gathers to say prayers, sing hymns, make offerings, hear a word, and share in the sacraments. Here we learn to live under and be interpreted by the stories, symbols, actions, and events which are the treasures of the church. Here our children, along with us, learn what it is to be, to become, and to do Christian as they actively engage in the community's worship.

The gathered congregation is the most visible model of the Christian church that our children—as well as we—have. How the community regards itself and its people provides children with clues, instructions, and directions as they develop understandings and feelings of themselves within the church. How the community approaches its tasks, does its worship, and regards and treats its children constitute basic instruction on the nature of the church. One thing is patently clear. The whole community, all of us together, is responsible for and involved in the Christian instruction, nurture, and growth of each other. As a model of what it is to be the church, the gathered, worshiping congregation is a teaching/learning environment. It is incumbent on us to utilize and maximize the opportunities present there.

Learning is social. Learning to be and do Christian, learning to do worship, is also social. As already suggested, we learn to be Christian only in community. There is no substitute for the experiences which children have most frequently in the family. What a child does with the family has special meaning and provides basic data and experiences for growth and maturity. What children do with their larger family, the church, can have special meaning and provide basic data and experiences for Christian growth and nurture. And what might children do with and in the larger family? To hear and be challenged by a word, to participate in an event, to be accepted and respected, to observe the faithful at work, to reflect upon and test out understandings and feelings—these are profound and critical experiences with the larger family. To say their prayers, to speak a word from the Lord, to share something of themselves, to do love, to give praise, and to make an offering—these our children can do with the larger family, enriching its total life while learning to be the family.

Focusing upon children's life in the larger family, we meet a most crucial issue, which calls forth our creative and innovative abilities. The opportunity for increased intergenerational interaction and activity is a pervasive need in the life of the church. There is the need that children, adolescents, and adults have the opportunity to interact and work with each other within the church; and the gathered, worshiping community can be a significant and primary locus for the interaction and activity.

Even as the gathered congregation is a model of the church, both adults and adolescents, collectively and individually, are faith-models for children. Regarded as models of doing worship and of what it means to be Christians, we offer powerful clues and instruction to our children. Children need models. But what do the models reveal? We must discover those ways by which all of us can speak a word of love, respect, and acceptance to the children, ways by which adults and adolescents may do an act of love or kindness and ways by which we can affirm our children as members of the household of faith.

Interaction has two directions. Not only do we share, but children share; not only do children receive, but we receive. From the children we can receive a word from the Lord; we can receive an act of love and kindness; we can receive new insight and understanding about our life together in the church. Above all, our children can share with us in doing the worship of the congregation, for it is their proper work also as members of the household of faith. So, all of us together learn to be the church.

They Participate as They Are Able

As children participate actively in the gathered community's worship, it is imperative that we neither demand nor expect them to do as adults or adolescents may be able. The worship they do and offer may lack much from the adult point of view. Nevertheless, it is their worship, the worship of Christian children, which is vitally important and necessary for the life of the gathered community.

Children do possess many abilities and capacities. At the same time their natural growth imposes limitations with which they necessarily live and work. How children grow in the faith is profoundly influenced by those limitations. Recognizing and appreciating those limitations we can assist our children to participate along with us in worship as they are able. We will not demand of them what they cannot do; we shall rejoice and delight in what they are able to do. Dealing sensitively with both the abilities and limitations of the children we can open for them new possibilities for life in the church.

All of us are engaged in an ongoing, complex, and difficult work of perceiving, organizing, and interpreting our world, making sense out of what is going on around us and giving meaning to the world, its events, ourselves, and our experiences. We are never done with this task which can be exciting and exhilarating, agonizing and frightening, all at the same time. Each of us is compelled to do that work for himself or herself. While it is a highly individualistic effort we do not engage in it in a vacuum or in isolation from others. We can do that task only in community. We absolutely need the assistance of others. Significant persons become our models, revealing modes of preceiving, organizing, and interpreting. A particular community to which we belong describes for us what is held to be true, good, and valuable, thus suggesting how we might organize and interpret our lives. Living in community, we achieve commonly shared interpretations, understandings, and meanings.

And so it is with our children. As deeply and earnestly as we might wish, we cannot deliver to them a ready-made world in any dimension. We cannot protect them from the hard work, the pain, and the failures experienced in the continuing work of perceiving, organizing, interpreting, and giving meaning. We can, however, assist them to engage in the task with delight, joy, and wonderment. The gathered, worshiping community can be an invaluable resource. Our children belong to the Christian community which perceives, organizes, and interprets the world and life in a particular manner rooted in a particular event. From within the community we can speak to our children a word, share with them our interpretations, challenge the adequacies of their understandings, and bring new experiences to bear upon their lives. We can engage them in the actions, events, and sacred texts of the faith. Thus, we join our children in their very human task, encouraging and challenging them to interpret their lives within the gathered community, even as that community has already interpreted them.

As they engage in the task, children work with significant

limitations. Let us consider here but briefly four limitations which impose restraints on children's abilities and capacities, noting the implications for children in the worshiping community. *First,* children work with particular and limited intellectual abilities. Preschool children regard themselves as the center of the world, possessing no effective way of "stepping outside" themselves so as to see themselves in some objective manner. Fantasy and fact blend together; the result becomes "truth." The thinking of preschool children is necessarily limited to concrete items and situations. In any given situation they most often focus on an insignificant or irrelevant item, making it the center of the situation and of their thinking. Limited to the insignificant they arrive at inadequate and inappropriate conclusion. They have no facility for making an intellectual check of the conclusion, but it stands as the "truth" of the situation. Moreover, they can deal with but one element of a situation at a given moment and have a marked inability to relate one item to another in any suitable manner. Intuitively, they draw conclusions from a single item, but rarely is there a necessary relationship between the two. Further, it is impossible for the preschool child to deal with abstract thinking as abstract thinking. Causal relationships are difficult to grasp. A sense of history and of the future is only rudimentary, if present at all.

Elementary children move to new intellectual possibilities in two significant dimensions. First, relational thinking, the ability to deal with two or more items of a situation in some logical manner, begins to emerge. Still unable to perform abstract thinking, they are able to relate two or more features of a situation to each other, thus producing more adequate conclusions. The thinking of elementary children is more complex than that of the preschoolers. Second, elementary children are able to make intellectual checks on their conclusions. They can work backwards from a conclusion, discovering if and where an error in thinking has been made. Both of these dimensions, however, are restricted to the concrete realm—concrete things and situations. Younger elementary children, in particular, are unable to think about ideas and encounter extreme difficulty in hypothetical, propositional thinking.

Second, we frequently fail to recognize a particular language limitation of children, with the result that we often make wrong conclusions concerning what children understand. Children's use of language far outstrips their understanding of that language. They can use a wide range of words with fluency but without understanding the significance or intent of the words. This is especially the case with connotative language, that which is highly analogical and metaphorical. While fluent in the use of words, children interpret them in a concretized and literalized manner. It is not until the end of elementary years that children begin to work effectively with analogical and metaphorical language. Nevertheless, we can deliberately condition children in the use of words. We must remember, however, that fluency in use is not to be equated with an understanding of the realities to which the words point. Otherwise, we will to quickly conclude that there is a particular understanding which in reality is not present.

Third, the range of children's experience is exceedingly far more narrow and restricted than that of adults. With the aid of our past experiences and our interpretations of them we meet and interpret new experiences. The larger our range of previous experiences and the more suitable our past interpretations the more possible it is to welcome new experiences and to make appropriate interpretations of them. Children are simply restricted in this domain, both in the range of experiences and in the practice of interpretations. Thus limited, they are simply unable to cope with certain experiences, often interpreting new experiences with naïve conclusions. They have no other alternatives. But given new experiences and the opportunity to practice interpretation they will attempt new conclusions.

Fourth, children, particularly preschoolers, have limited ability to take on the thinking and feeling of others or to put themselves consciously into the shoes of another person. They cannot enter deeply into the intentions and thinking of others and are unable to describe with some precision the feelings of another. Interpretations of others' feelings and intentions are primarily reflections of the children's egocentrism in which they are bound. Verbal appeals to a concept of altruism based upon how another person feels quite often miss the mark with preschool children. Elementary children, however, are somewhat more proficient in the task of role-taking. While much of that task is yet to be learned, they are beginning to enter into the perspective of another's thinking and feeling. But still they have not learned to see themselves through the eyes of another person.

These four limitations have significant and far-reaching implications for our life with children in the gathered, worshiping
community. Following sections will discuss the implications in some
detail. Thus, only a brief discussion is necessary here. *First,* we must
provide opportunities for children to articulate verbally their
perceiving, organizing, and interpreting of the world, its events,
experiences, and people. Those articulations, with their accompa-
nying interpretations, will be immature, naïve, and greatly lacking
from an adult point of view. Nevertheless, we must encourage the
children to do what they are able to do. It is critical that we accept the
articulations and interpretations as serious attempts by the children
to come to terms with the world and their life in it.

Their articulations will reflect both intellectual abilities and
limitations. Hearing a Bible story, younger children especially will
most often focus on an insignificant, even trivial, item of the story.
Further, they regard that item as the totality of the story. From the
insignificant they intuitively arrive at conclusions, and those
conclusions stand as the "truth" of the story. The children make
interpretations that are immature, naïve, and even bizarre,
interpretations which have little to do with the intent of the story. We
need not be embarrassed by any interpretation given; we need not
make more of the interpretation than is present. Listening attentively
and sensitively to children's interpretations, we can determine a new
word to be spoken, a new question to be asked, and a new experience
to be given. Thus, we can challenge the children to make new
interpretations, yet never demanding more than they are capable of
achieving. The opportunities that are afforded in the gathered
community encourage the children to practice the work of
interpretation even as they are interpreting their lives with and
within a community of God's people.

Second, we can share the particularity of the Christian community
as it organizes and interprets the world and life through language.
Children can easily learn to use the religious language in phrases and
sentences. Much of Christian education has been a deliberate
attempt to condition children in the use of religious language. We
dare not conclude too much from that usage, for children do not have
the ability to work effectively and appropriately with much of the
religious language, especially the analogical and metaphorical. Yet
they should have the opportunity to work with and explore that

language. They will not understand much of its intent as adults may. Thus, recognizing children's tendency to concretize and literalize language, we must make attempts to use words attuned to their abilities and limitations. Our language with children should not be argumentative, propositional, or embedded with complex explanations. Certainly we cannot and should not avoid our significant religious language. So, simple, declarative statements will be spoken, frequently without explanation. Our use of the faith's language ought to be a model for the children as they learn to use the language.

Third, we can share the particularity of the Christian community not only through language but in common experiences shared within the gathered congregation. We can provide a wide and generous range of experiences which will not only enrich the lives of the children but ours also, both immediately and for the future. The experiences provided are not solely for the children. They are to be experiences in which all of us together can share in common. And if they are not experiences involving the whole community, they are nothing more than "operations" performed on the children by adults.

At the same time, our children need the freedom and leisure to explore their own lives within the community as they encounter the church's sacred texts, symbols, stories, and events. Their interpretations of a Bible story may be naïve, marked by gross anthropomorphisms; their prayers may ramble disconnectedly, replete with magical incantations; their offerings will be simple. Yet, in such efforts our children, consciously or unconsciously, are exploring as they are able what it means to be Christian and what it is to do worship. They are learning to worship. Anxious as we may be to move them along, to speed the process, the children can proceed only as they are able. We must give them the leisure and space in which to explore, while challenging and pushing when appropriate. Yet they are children doing worship and learning to worship; they are learning to be and do Christian. As we participate along with the children in the exploration, we encourage and assist the children, and all of us together, in the ongoing task of interpreting life from within a community of God's people.

Fourth, children's great difficulty in assuming the perspective of another directs many of our efforts. We cannot expect them, with precision, to describe how a biblical character may have felt or thought. What we may hear, however, are the feeling and thinking of the children themselves. Verbal exhortations to love and kindness will have little, if any, effect in and of themselves. The proposition that we should or can love our neighbor because God first loved us will lose its power with the children. The verbal exhortation coupled with an action behavior, however, can be a profound and significant event for the children and the entire congregation. Within the gathered community children can do love, can do kindness. We can engage children in doing the behaviors which belong to the community even as we identify them with our verbal behavior.

An additional comment concerning behaviors must be made here. Our participation in various behaviors influences greatly how we go about the task of perceiving, organizing, and interpreting. It is desirable and most necessary that we engage the children, as they are able, in the behaviors which belong to the Christian community. Using a community's particular language is a behavior. Thinking is a behavior. Doing Christian is a behavior. Worship is a behavior. We can engage the children in the behaviors of the gathered, worshiping community. They can pray; they can speak a word from God; they can do praise, they can do love; they can make an offering. In short, they can do worship, behaving as the worshiping community.

And One Last Long Note

Children are limited in their cognitive understanding of the faith's language, its symbol system and sacred texts, the profundity of its actions and the complexity of its values. Greater cognitive understanding is a future possibility, and we can make contributions to that future reality as we provide a wide and generous range of experiences. There is, also, an affective dimension to understanding. Children know with clarity and exactness how they are regarded and treated. They know when they have been included or excluded, though they may not have the slightest notion of the why. They learn quickly "their place." The gathered community is the children's most visible model of the church; its adult members are faith-models. The models, positive or negative, are observable. Enthusiasm in worship, overt expressions of moods, treatment of others, postures and gestures in worship, and even the preaching event—these are observable and can be imitated. Children, imitating their models, seek to make sense out of what is going on around them, attempt to discover their place in the community, and learn to be and do Christian. Imitation of the community's life may stimulate our children in the joy and excitement of new feelings and thinking, of celebration and participation. Thus, we must ask, What model do we offer for imitation? But children are not involved in sheer imitation. Doing the behaviors which belong to the community, they are the community.

Our children belong in and with the gathered, worshiping community. There, as in no other place, they receive the affirmation of who they already are. There they are surrounded by the words, events, symbols, and actions which identify them. There they do worship even as they learn to worship. There they do Christian even as they learn to become Christian. Whatever we do along with children in worship must not isolate or exclude but plunge them into the very center of the community's life and work, encouraging and enabling their active participation as they are able.

II. Enabling Active Participation

II. Enabling Active Participation

In every facet of ministry it is essential that we place upon ourselves realistic demands and expectations. It is crucial that we have some clear recognition of what we may or may not be able to accomplish, learning to work within necessary bounds and being done with the impossible. Failing to make such distinctions, we burden ourselves unnecessarily with frustration and failure. So, as we ask, What can we do *along with* children in worship? we need clarity of expectations within the range of the possible.

Let us cast off a particular intolerable and unnecessary burden. It is not our task to "make Christians" of our children. We simply cannot achieve that work. We cannot assure anyone through word or deed that our children will always remain within the Christian community. No work on our part can produce such an assurance. But let us give our attention and efforts to what we can do.

We can so arrange our life in the gathered, worshiping community that major, powerful contributions can be made for Christian growth and nurture. We can so arrange our life together that an exciting, stimulating, and abundant range of opportunities is offered, inviting and enabling the children to share in the community's worship. We can provide an environment which will assist and encourage our children to interpret their lives with and within the Christian community.

This book presents a series of strategies which can be realized in the worshiping community. The strategies suggest new arrangements of our life together. Effecting them we will graciously invite the children, along with us, to share in the stories, actions, words, and symbols which identify all of us as Christians. Responding to the invitation, the children along with us will participate actively in the worship of the gathered congregation.

The strategy descriptions are marked by a number of characteristics and are informed by particular assumptions and understandings. The content of each description is obviously important, but the force and impact of the strategies will not be realized through mere use of content. It is essential that we give deliberate attention to those characteristics, assumptions, and understandings and their implications, bringing them into play as we implement the strategies. In so doing, we will enable our children to do the worship of the gathered congregation.

Children's Experience: The Beginning Point

The children's experience, not content and not our agenda, is the beginning point of each strategy. Most of the children's experiences occur in a much larger arena than the gathered community. Collectively, they compose the "familiar" for the children. They are the "stepping-stones" by which children remain in touch with the familiar while daring to venture into the unfamiliar. Whatever new experiences we offer must be somewhat related to the previous ones. If not, we involve them in events and activities which are senseless and useless to them.

As persons engaged in the ongoing task of interpretation, children do make interpretations of their past experiences. In that activity they are giving meaning to their life, attempting to make sense of it and, in a most profound sense, creating "reality." Their intepretations constitute the "real world" for them. Children approach all new experiences, at least initially, from within the content and interpretation of previous ones.

Each strategy identifies an experience familiar to most children, using it as the base for building and introducing new experiences. Equally important, we need to know how our children have interpreted their past experiences. We need to know how they understand and feel about not only their experiences but themselves, their world, their life in community, God, and Jesus. Within the gathered community, we need to know how they are interpreting the content of the faith at a given time. With that knowledge we can move with some confidence in providing new experiences which will challenge the children to new understandings. How are we to know these things? We ask the children. Given the opportunity in an environment of respect and acceptance, the children will share much with us.

The children need the freedom to talk; they need attentive, respectful listeners. What they share with us is important to them; it is a part of them. They are telling us how they "put the world together." They are telling us what "sense" they make of things. From the adult view, it may all sound very strange, confused, funny, inadequate, trite, and even blatantly wrong. But they are doing the best they can. Thus, we will not laugh at or ridicule what is shared with us. We will not dismiss it as merely childish. We will not be bound by the compulsion to make "corrections." For us to declare an understanding "wrong" will be of little value and will not necessarily serve to correct. Such an action on our part will simply cause the children to be reluctant in sharing with us. What they share with us is to be regarded with respect. They need assurance and experience in taking the risk of sharing.

Without any question whatsoever, we will not leave the children as victims of their own mistakes. We will not reinforce inadequate understanding through benign indulgence. With a knowledge of the children's past experiences and present interpretations, we can provide new experiences within the context and content of the gathered community, experiences impinging upon and challenging the past while urging and encouraging children to dare an encounter with the unfamiliar.

The strategies suggest numerous ways by which we can provide a rich and generous range of experiences within the gathered community. We can speak a new word, tell a story, ask a question, or have a parade. Such may prompt the children to ask anew, "What's it all about?" Even as we share our understandings and feelings, not as final answers but as a talking together in the faith, we provide new experiences. Our sharing provides new challenges and problems requiring new solutions. We can effect those events and situations which may stimulate the children's sense of wonder to come alive, thus encouraging the journey from the familiar to the unfamiliar.

How Much Content?

In educational ministry with children, we are constantly plagued by the question: How much explicit content of the faith do we present to children? The same question presents itself here. As responsible persons, we must give a response. As we implement the strategies, we must work with several contents. Already noted, the children's past experiences and interpretations constitute the initial content of the strategies. Essential and necessary as this may be it is not sufficient for our task. New experiences within the gathered worshiping community will be additional content. Even though those experiences may be the most influential, dominant, and informative

21

content that many children will receive concerning the faith, something more is necessary.

We meet the children within the gathered, worshiping community, a community informed and shaped by particular stories, sacred texts, symbols, actions, and values. If our children are to learn to interpret their lives from within the faith even as the faith interprets them, the content of the faith must be brought to bear upon them. None of us can interpret, act upon, or make sense of what is not available to us. So it is with the content of the faith. Recognizing the limitations within which children work, we must ask: When and under what circumstances is the content of the faith available to children?

Availability of content is not to be defined by the quantity of information given. We can give an abundance of information which remains absolutely unavailable to the children intellectually, affectively, and experientially. With their limitations and narrow range of experience they cannot deal effectively and adequately with the intent of such information. Equally significant, unavailable information is useless to the children and may create unnecessary difficulties. In Christian education, we often behave as if our job is to transmit as early as possible large quantities of correct information which, we assume, will prevent or eliminate all mistakes. The history of Christian education provides ample proof of the fallacy of any such assumption. Mistakes have not been eliminated or prevented. Quite to the contrary, an oversupply of information, as well as information unavailable intellectually, affectively, and experientially, are frequently the sources of confusion. They make possible and encourage mistakes, the very thing we hope to avoid.

We are all familiar with the continuing debate relative to the value of memorization. We have heard it many times. We know the argument that biblical stories and passages memorized in childhood, even without an understanding of their intent, will be of great value to the individual in adulthood. There is mounting evidence to suggest that the assertion is simply not correct. Rather, there is evidence that mere memorization of religious material may interfere with, disrupt, and make difficult Christian growth and nurture. Religious material merely memorized frequently leads to confusion rather than clarification. It contributes to gross and naïve mistakes in interpretation. Under no circumstances should we add unnecessarily to the difficulties that children have with religious content.

Let us not be concerned primarily with the quantity of religious content given. Large amounts of religious information imposed upon children are neither desirable nor useful. The strategies in the last part of this book identify various contents of the faith with the understanding that they are available to the children intellectually, affectively, and experientially. The children, within their abilities, limitations, and range of experience, can come to useful, significant encounters with that content. It may be a Bible story, a single biblical sentence, a simple declarative statement, exploration of one word, or an activity. It may be but a simple assurance of love, a faith-statement without explanation, or a "verbal pointer," a statement directing attention to some item or feature of a story or an event.

No longer focusing upon the amount of content given, we can offer an opportunity and a freedom to the children. The children need the opportunity to act upon the content given, to think about it, to respond to it, to ask questions of it, and to explore it, making and testing interpretations. The same content we will bring to bear on many occasions in varying ways. The children need the freedom to work with that content not as adults but as they are able, learning to claim it as their own. They need freedom to risk mistakes even as they are learning to be the church. And, strangely but wonderfully, in turn we are granted a freedom and opportunity. We are free of the unnecessary burden to demand "right" answers, a demand which serves to rob the children of the adventure in exploration and discovery. And we have the opportunity to listen, receiving joyfully what the children share with us.

The language of the faith is content of the faith. With care and deliberateness we are to bring that language to bear upon the children. To use the language of the faith appropriately is both desirable and necessary. To learn the appropriate use of the faith's language is to learn to think well about the faith. Learning to use language is also learning to think. We have discussed earlier children's fluent use of religious words and the mistaken conclusions to which it can lead us. With the warnings and possible pitfalls, we will engage the children in the language of the faith. We will explore with the children what they understand the language to be about, always pointing them to new possibilities. The strategies presented give focus to the language of the faith and its use. In them, the language of the faith has been selected carefully and deliberately. It is language available to the children, language upon which they can act appropriately, use in doing worship, and employ in interpreting their lives within the Christian community. Our use of the faith's language with the children is of crucial significance. Our use is a model for the children, not only as a description of how and when the language is used but as a way of thinking about the faith.

Assistance in Reflection and Interpretation

Throughout our discussion thus far, there has been an emphasis on the tasks of reflection and interpretation. The discussion and the strategies presented in this book insist that within the context and content of the gathered, worshiping community children should be encouraged and assisted to reflect, as they are able, upon their experiences, feelings, thinking and understandings. Only as reflection occurs in the content and context of the community will the children be enabled to interpret their lives within the faith. Reflection and interpretation are learned. Learning those tasks, though rudimentary at first, can begin early. From reflection flow new feelings, new interpretations, new doings, and new arrangements of the world. An implementation of the strategies will assist the learning of reflection and interpretation in several ways.

First, the strategies encourage that we give ample opportunity for the children to give verbal articulation to their feeling, thinking, experiences, and information. Their verbal articulations will be not only reflective of how they understand the world but will be efforts, in themselves, to make sense of their lives. Attempting such articulation, the children come to larger understandings of themselves and the world. They are engaged in the tasks of reflection and interpretation. At the same time, they hear themselves talking. In so doing children frequently make correction, attempt new starts, and produce new responses. Hearing oneself talk often stimulates new thinking and feeling. The opportunity for attempting verbal articulation is crucial in the work of learning reflection and interpretation.

While children learn from hearing themselves talk, they also learn from hearing each other talk. Children listening to other children discover clues to their own speaking and thinking. They discover a new solution to a problem. They learn to look at a situation in a new way. Children help each other in sorting out problems and situations while challenging the thinking of each other. As adults, we engage in the same process. Yet, there is a particular aspect of children helping children which we must appreciate and use. Frequently, children can help each other to identify a problem or mistake as adults cannot. Listening to how other children view and solve a problem, a child may receive intellectually, affectively, and experientially available clues for further solutions, reflections, and interpretations. Implementing the strategies we will encourage and assist the children to talk with each other, enabling them to help each other in the tasks of reflection and interpretation.

We noted earlier that learning to use appropriately the language of the faith assists in learning to think appropriately about the faith. Children need both the guidance and practice in articulating the faith's language. They can discuss the community's actions, its symbols and sacred texts, and thus they engage in reflection and interpretation. As they say their prayers, they do worship while learning to do worship. With guidance they can speak a word from God, while yet learning how to speak that word. As they share their verbal expression, they contribute to the whole community and have an investment in what is taking place, while yet learning to be the community. Working with the language of the faith, they engage in the work of reflection and interpretation even as they are being interpreted by that language.

Second, reflection and interpretation can be facilitated greatly by questions asked. To ask questions of others concerning their thinking and feeling is to produce new challenges, arousing new reflections and calling forth new articulations and interpretations. The strategies rely heavily upon the question-asking process, a process requiring careful, deliberate, and sensitive execution.

As the question-makers we will not play games with the children. The game, "Guess what I am thinking and you will be right," must have no place among us. That games focuses upon us and the information we wish to impart rather than upon the children. Questions which begin with "Don't you think . . . ?" may elicit what we judge to be a correct answer, but they stifle and interfere with reflection, exploration, and interpretation. They seduce children into giving answers sensed to be pleasing to us.

Our questions should encourage and elicit from the children expressions of their thinking and feeling, while serving as challenges to new reflection and interpretation. "Why do you think that?" "Why do you feel that way?" "Will you tell me more about that?" "How would you think or feel if . . .?" "Are there some other things that you think about that?" Such questions give freedom and space in which the children work while proposing new solutions, considering new problems, and testing understandings. They assist children in making distinctions, clarifying interpretations, making decisions, and venturing from the familiar to the unfamiliar.

As models for asking questions, we can help the children learn the art of asking questions. In turn, they will propose questions to us. In the interaction between us and the children, they are at work in the arena of reflection and interpretation. In that arena they may grasp the first understandings that the work of reflection and interpretation is an ongoing process, never finished but always exciting and expanding.

Not all children will be able to respond to probing and prodding questions with equal ease and facility. They may lack the practice necessary. They may be restrained by the desire to give the "right" answer. So we will be patient with the children as they learn to take the risk of responding openly and freely, approaching the work of reflection and interpretation.

Intergenerational Interaction

An increased intergenerational activity, as noted earlier, is a pervasive need of the church. Sharing in the celebrations of the gathered community, children along with the adults learn to be and to do who they already are. In community we do worship; in community we learn to do worship. In the gathered congregation our children are with men and women who can affirm them as God's people and share faith and life. Equally, the children can do the same for the adults.

The strategies in this book suggest a number of activities which will facilitate intergenerational interaction. The children may move throughout the congregation, speaking a word of God, giving a kiss or hug, proclaiming a blessing, sharing such a simple thing as a flower, leading a parade, or welcoming a new member into the community. They may do the worship of the congregation in prayer, dance, praise, or an offering. In those activities, the adults can share. They can greet the children in joy and celebration. They can do acts of love and kindness. They can give a kiss or a hug. They can speak a word. They can join a parade.

Doubtless, we shall need to assist the adults to share in the worship which the children do. We will share with them our understanding of worship and the intent of what is occurring. We will ask for their cooperation and participation. We will not ask them to patronize but to greet and receive the children as members of the household of faith. And so, all of us together can do and learn the proper work of the gathered community.

The usefulness and force of the strategies in this book depend significantly upon those who implement them. It is suggested that the pastor be the responsible person. The strategies, themselves, are descriptions of interaction between the pastor and children. Pastors are powerful, influential faith-models for children. Frequently, the pastor stands in God's place. The actions of the pastor are often regarded as the actions of God. How the pastor regards and treats the children may constitute initial understanding of how God regards and treats them. Also, from a serious interaction between the pastor and children a profound and abiding pastoral relationship can emerge.

In our interactions with the children there shall be demands and expectations which we can meet directly and simply, giving freedom, space, encouragement, and new possibilities. As already discussed, with all of our "right" answers we cannot "tinker around" in the lives of children, or of anyone else, ordering and reordering their thinking, understanding, and feelings. But we can share ourselves with them. We can indicate which character in a Bible story we like the most. We can speak of the things we hold to be important and beautiful. We can describe how we have felt and acted on an occasion. We can speak of our love and of God's love for them. Our sharing, presented not as complete, final, and finished answers, becomes new experiences and content, opening rich possibilities for reflection and growth within the gathered community.

The implementation of any one strategy will entail much conversation between the pastor and children. In some detail we will discuss, shortly, the work of conversing with children. Several comments, however, are in order here. In our conversations with the children we will encounter surprising and unanticipated statements and answers. Children's simple, even naïve, responses will often be disarming. We need not be embarrassed by the content of their conversation. We need not move too quickly to "hush them up" or to judge rightness or wrongness. Rather, we will use each conversation as a new occasion for the continuing question: What, now, are the activities, verbal pointers, stories, or questions which will encourage and assist the children to reflect anew upon their lives within the gathered community?

The strategies outline various activities in which the children will participate. We will give directions, but more will be expected of us. We will join with the children even as we encourage others to join. We will join the parade, join in a proclamation, share in their prayers, dance with them, or do an act of love.

Our implementation of strategies shall demand of us a posture of openness and acceptance—an openness to any expression and an acceptance of its importance to the child; a willingness to share—a sharing of our understandings and feelings with the children and a gracious reception of what the children share with us; and a flexibility and spontaneity—a flexibility encouraging the children to set something of the agenda and a spontaneity of response to the unexpected. The children will join us enthusiastically and encourage us in such a posture.

Active, Not Passive, Participation

Our entire discussion here is a clear and needed challenge to the church. It is a direct and unequivocal call to the church: let us encourage and enable our children's active participation in the celebrations of the congregation so that all of us together may do the worship of the Christian community. Much of what we have done *for* the children in worship has cast them into the role of passive recipients of our activities. Such a result may not have been our intention in the least, but intention is not in question here. Try as we may we cannot give or transmit to our children a ready-made faith. Given the opportunities to act upon, to react to, and to engage in the activities and life of the gathered community, our children will be enabled to claim the faith and the life of the community as their own possession. They will be assisted to do and to learn the worship of the community. They will enter upon the adventure of becoming and doing who they already are.

As responsible persons in the life of the church, we ought to make every effort to enable the active participation of children in the life and celebration of the community. Our implementation of the strategies in this book will be one effort to encourage not only the children but the whole congregation into active participation. Some avenues open to us have been suggested, and the strategy descriptions identify more. To speak a word, to give expression to thinking and feeling, to share a flower, to give a kiss, to enter a parade, to greet another, to pray, to give praise, and to make an offering—these are active engagements in the life of the community. They are behaviors which belong to the whole people of God.

Not all children will participate actively in the same manner in each experience or event suggested in the strategies; not all will be captivated or stimulated equally by all parts of a strategy. Timidity and shyness may interfere. Interests may move in a diversity of directions. Past experiences may not be sufficient. Natural abilities and limitations will be determining factors. We cannot expect the same things from all the children at the same time. And so we go full circle to the beginning of this chapter. We will give our time, energy, and efforts to those things which are possible. we can arrange and create an environment, our life in community, which invites and encourages our children, as they are able, to do and learn worship along with us all together.

III. On Implementing the Strategies

III. On Implementing the Strategies

The strategies presented in the following section are collectively but one response to the question: What can we do *along with* children in worship? They are offered in a conviction informed by experience in congregational settings that our children, along with all of us, can do the worship of the gathered community. But a danger is ever present. What is proposed as an exciting and dynamic approach to a longstanding problem can sink quickly and easily into routine, triviality, and boredom if appropriate and sufficient time and care are not exercised. A quick glance at the strategies may lead to the mistaken conclusion that they are highly formal and rigid, requiring extensive planning and an excessive investment of time. Certainly, as persons concerned about the worship of the community, we will expect to invest time and energy.

More important than the amount of time and energy devoted will be our commitment to the particular approach and understanding of the task which we have been discussing. Recalling the earlier discussions, we will work to develop and create an environment in which the realization of certain possibilities may be maximized. Some adjustments and rearrangements of our life together will be required. Some different use of time will be necessary. Such tasks will be relatively easy and simple, yet thrilling and joyous, when we agree to greet our children as members of the household of faith whose rightful place is in the gathered, worshiping community.

Responding to the Local Situation

Perhaps, at their best, the strategies are clues and guidelines to be employed in a critical work of the church. They are points of departure. They are not offered as complete and final procedures to be followed slavishly in every detail, promising always "positive" and "desirable" results. They are not final answers to be imposed upon a worshiping community. Approaching them from such a stance, we will reduce them to the routine and trivial.

The strategies are but suggestions which are to be given form and specificity as the local situation makes possible. The physical layout of the worship area will influence activities and events initiated. The size of the congregational membership, including the number of children, may impose particular limits on strategy implementations. Already-held attitudes concerning children's presence in the congregation will suggest the strategies to be used initially and the frequency of their implementation. The past experiences of the children in the gathered community will guide our interaction. The location of the congregation—rural, urban, or suburban—will offer rich and particular content to the strategies. In short, the strategies presented serve as models for generating and building new possibilities, attuned to the local situation.

Predicting Directions

Encouraging significant interaction, free conversation, and physical activity, we will be unable to predict every turn and direction that a strategy may take. Our lack of predictive ability need not bother us unduly. Let us remember that the children are determining something of the agenda. Their needs and interests at the moment may be more critical than our agenda. To our agenda we can return at another time. The imagination and wonderment of the children may lead us in unanticipated yet exciting directions. Unexpected twists and turns will be encouraged and welcome. Obviously, order, even within a wide range of freedom, must be present. The strategy descriptions give practical directions which will assist us "to swing with" the children and give guidance to their interests and concerns. As we work over a period of time with the strategies, we will learn from practice. Our predictive abilities will be increased and sharpened. But let us enjoy, welcome, and expect children who will continue to challenge us with the unanticipated, leading us to new interactions, insights, and understandings.

A New Order of Things

Even with a quick reading of the strategies we recognize that implementation will not only disturb the normal flow of most worship services but require some alterations in the usual order, a different use of time, and a new understanding of what is "permissible" during worship. The shifts or alterations will not be great, but we are aware that in many situations even a slight change in worship order can cause much difficulty. So again, we must alert the entire congregation to the intent and significance of the task, asking not merely for quiet tolerance but for active involvement.

First, no one location in the worship service is suitable for all strategies. One may be implemented at the beginning of the service, another replacing a hymn, one at the sermon, another at the offering, and another during the congregational prayer. And still another may be used at several points within a single service. The aim and content of each strategy will suggest a possible location, and we should not hestitate to experiment in this matter.

Second, we will make new use and allocations of time. Clearly, we are not discussing an investment of "two or three minutes with the children." Some strategies will require five to ten minutes, some even a bit more. There may not be an easy solution to the problem of time. A longer service? A shorter sermon? One less hymn? Perhaps a strategy may be used in lieu of the regular sermon. The decision will be made in the local situation. Clearly, a suitable investment of time is necessary if the force and intent of the strategies are to be realized. We must not hurry, impatient to get on to another agenda. Practice with the strategies will enable us to judge more accurately the time necessary.

Third, implementing the strategies we will encourage some things which have been discouraged during worship services. Much conversation, shouting, laughter, and many questions will occur. Body movements and physical activity will increase. A new and higher level of noise will result. We will keep some control of the events; they need not get out of hand. But even as we take care the quiet, solemn, and well-ordered service will be disturbed—and maybe some adults. Even the janitor may be upset on occasion by a bit of mess left behind. But with all the risks and difficulties involved in a new order of things, perhaps our worship together can be celebration.

On Using Strategy Descriptions

The strategy descriptions are offered as models, as points of departure, and not as detailed plans to be followed without variation. They reflect the experiences of the authors in actual congregational settings. They contain parts of actual conversations with children. They alert us to possible difficult areas, pitfalls, and unexpected questions and turns along the way. The text of the strategy descriptions is of three kinds.

First, there are statements of aim, descriptions of materials needed, preparations to be made, and suggestions relative to age suitability and location in the service. It is imperative that we have a clear, precise aim for what we are doing. If not, we will find ourselves moving in many directions all at the same time, not quite knowing where we are going and creating confusion for the children. Whatever our aim or objective it must be a possibility for the children. We ought not to ask them to do what they cannot do. Oftentimes our well-developed and proper aims will not be totally realized. The children, with their needs, experiences, and interests, will set new agendas. In those unexpected turns, we can still assist the children to do the worship of the church and to interpret their lives within the community. To our specific agenda we can return at another time.

Second, the major portion of the descriptions is written as the pastor's involvement in conversation with the children. As the implementation unfolds and takes shape, our conversations will not conform in all details to the text given here. Further, nothing is to be gained in working for a conformity. Rather, the major thrusts of the texts are to demonstrate language which is appropriate, useful, and available to children, to highlight the use of questions, and to illustrate the sequencing of materials, questions, and activities.

Third, the text within parentheses presents a number of directions and guidelines for our use. It suggests ways to bring children into active participation, to alter unexpected turns, and to deal sensitively with the children without embarrassment to them. It includes comments and responses made by children in actual congregational settings, and these alert us to potentially difficult areas.

How Much of Each Strategy?

In implementing the strategies we need not attempt to employ every item at a given time. Most descriptions contain more suggestions and materials than can be adequately used on one occasion. We will need to make our own choices. Some items can be omitted without interfering with the strategy's intent. Time restraints may occasion some deletions; children's interests and needs may require more time devoted to an item than had been expected. The critical issue is not the amount of material we are able to cover. Rather, when deletions are made, we should make every effort to retain the basic characteristics of the strategies discussed earlier.

Some strategy descriptions include suggested variations for a particular thrust or theme. Though not developed in detail, the variations offer clues for the building of additional events. In fact, a variation may be preferred over the detailed description and can be developed within the particularity of the local situation.

Having implemented a strategy we need not relegate it to the past or regard it as completed. The impact of a strategy is not spent in one use. The dynamic characteristics of the strategies, the continuing development of the children, and the richness of the faith's content urge us to repeat, periodically, the same strategy with the same children. No two implementations will take the same turns and directions. Variations can be added to repeated uses. Certainly, the same strategy can be used with groups of children varying in age.

On Age Grouping

The strategies are designed for use with preschool and elementary children. As already noted, among these children are wide differences in abilities and experiences. A particular strategy will not assist, encourage, and excite all children equally. Not all children can participate in each with the same ability, interest, or understanding. Not expecting the same thing from all the children, we will encourage their participation as they are able.

Some strategies are more suitable for the preschool child, others for the elementary child. Notations on suitability are made at the end of each strategy description. Those notations alert us to the appropriate expectations that we might have of the children. If the group is composed of both preschool and elementary children, we can anticipate a wide and varying range of participation and understanding. We will encounter questions and responses which reflect the wide age-span. Confronted by a wide and varied range of abilities and experiences, we will not permit the older children to dominate the situation. Nevertheless, we can involve both preschool and elementary children together. Children of varying ages working together can contribute richly to the learning and doing of each other.

In congregations with large numbers of children, we will not be able to implement strategies including all the children at one time. Large numbers will militate against the active participation urged by the strategies. Working with a rather large group, we may encounter difficulty exercising reasonable control over activities, body movements, and noise. On a given Sunday we may invite only the preschool children or only the elementary children to participate. Other small groupings are possible, such as first and second graders or third and fourth graders. Using age groupings we should not hesitate to repeat a strategy with several groups.

On Conversing with Children

Close encounters with children in conversation can be frightening. Children's simple, open, and even naïve comments and questions can unnerve us. Their unexpected responses can disarm us. Conversing, in a sense, is an art which can be developed and learned through practice. What can be a frightening, unnerving, and disarming experience can become a thrilling, exciting, and enriching adventure. Conversing with the children, we will be guided by several concerns.

First, our language and its intent must be available to the children intellectually, affectively, and experientially. To talk down to children is demeaning of them; to talk above them is to miss the mark with them. Our language with them will be simple and direct. It will challenge but not overwhelm. It will give clues to insight and understanding without imposing closures to exploration and discovery. It will be descriptive and declarative, unencumbered by complicated explanations. The directions we give will be simple, describing clearly what we want to occur. Repeated directions can be most helpful to the children.

Second, children will use religious language in peculiar, even funny, ways without significant understanding of its intent. It is vitally important to their life in the church that they learn *when* and *how* to use that language appropriately. We can challenge their use of language with a question as simple as, "Will you tell me more about that?" Such a question will encourage and aid the children to reflect upon what they have said. Occasionally we will invite the children to speak a sentence to the congregation. In so doing we will provide opportunity for the children both to do what Christians do and to learn *when* and *how* to use the church's language. In addition, our simple, descriptive, and declarative use of the language will be a model for the children as they learn an essential task.

Third, in conversation children frequently share spontaneously events, language, and behaviors which emerge from their families. Some of the information, spread before the congregation, may be a source of embarrassment and discomfort for parents. The children are sharing what is important to them. They are attempting to make sense of what is going on around them. To chide them for their efforts will not be helpful but destructive. Still, we will not add to the embarrassment and discomfort of parents by focusing on sensitive information. A simple "I understand what you are saying," or "Yes, that's happened to me also," or "We will talk about that later" will suffice. If we suggest a later conversation, it is imperative that we return to the child individually in a different context. In our conversations we may encounter other "sensitive" information which does not emerge from the family. We need not be embarrassed by it, but we will deal with it carefully and kindly.

Fourth, we will ask many questions of the children. In time, they will ask questions of us. When children attempt and formulate questions, they are grasping for understanding. We will not be too quick to respond with answers but will often ask the children to attempt answers to their own questions. How they formulate their questions and the answers to them gives us new information about the children. We learn the "real" question they are asking; we learn how they see the world. With such knowledge, we will pose new questions which can assist in clarification. To our discomfort at times, children will ask the impossible question, the question for which we have no answers. In such instances, we share with them something of our understanding of the issue at hand. It is neither necessary nor possible that we have final answers to all questions. Of course we will frequently answer children's questions directly. But our responses must serve the needs of the children, not our need to give answers.

Children can be spontaneous in word and action. They can surprise us. They do not respect the "social niceties" of conversation. We can dare to take the risk of a "disaster" on occasion. We can, also, dare take the risk of sharing joyfully and thankfully with the children as they do worship even as they are learning to do worship.

Within the Church Year

The strategy descriptions are organized within the Christian church year, with many included under the heading, "Life in the Church." Various strategies are suitable as we move from Advent through Pentecost and Trinity Sunday and are so noted. Some do not make overt verbal reference to the particular season. Some of us may wish to identify more specifically the season or occasion. In so doing we should give a simple "name" or identification without involved explanations. With or without the verbal identifications, the strategies reflect the seasons, great events, and celebrations of the Christian church and involve the children in them.

It is not necessary to use the strategy descriptions at only one particular time of the year. With some variation and flexibility, we can use a single strategy several times within a year. Thus, specific contents of the faith will be repeated. In repetition, the children will have new opportunities to act upon and react to that content. No two implementations of the same strategy will be identical. Learning to work well with a relatively limited range of content is far more desirable than overwhelming children with an oversupply of information.

Some strategies are similar in directions, content, and intent and deliberately so. Similarity of strategies builds an arena of the familiar which can assist the children to risk the unfamiliar. Overarching the particularity of each strategy is a single intent: to help the children along with us of all ages to do the worship of the gathered Christian community. So, come, let us worship together.

IV. Come, Let Us Worship Together

We Tell About Jesus

Aim: To enable the children to speak (sing) a word about Jesus to the congregation.

Material: A simple song about Jesus which may be used with a guitar, autoharp, piano, or organ. (Make arrangements for the musical accompaniment. The refrain of "Go Tell It on the Mountain" is a suitable hymn selection.)

1. How many of you know about Jesus? Tell us some of the things that you know about Jesus. (Give the children ample opportunity for talking. Responses will be greatly varied. The children may use a lot of religious language, the intent of which they may not understand. There is no need or value in attempting to "correct" the children by giving additional language. Some responses will be "funny." Do not laugh at responses.)

2. How did you learn about Jesus? (This may be a difficult question for the younger children, and some may respond, "I just did," or, "I got it out of my head.") Who helps you to learn about Jesus? (Church school teachers, parents, minister in the sermon, choir in its singing. Some children may identify the Bible. Acknowledge that contribution but keep the focus on persons.)

3. Yes, there are many people who tell us about Jesus. And you, too, can tell others about Jesus. You can help others learn about Jesus.

4. A moment ago we mentioned that the choir in hymns, songs, and anthems tells us about Jesus. Today I want you to be a choir and tell our friends about Jesus. I have here the words to a short hymn or song which tells about Jesus. Let us learn the song and then sing it for others in the congregation. (Teach the song. Have the children face the congregation and sing.)

5. Good! Now you have told others about Jesus. You have helped us learn about Jesus. Now let's ask our friends in the congregation to sing the song with us. (Repeat the words. Encourage the entire congregation to sing.)

6. As we have all sung together, we have told each other about Jesus.

Variations:

a) The focus could be on the Bible as the book which tells us stories about Jesus. The children could learn a verse to be spoken to the congregation.

b) If the strategy is used during the Advent season, a simple reference to John the Baptist as one who told others of Jesus would be most appropriate.

Age suitability: Preschool and elementary.

An Advent Offering

Aim: To enable the children to do an act of love in the Advent season.

Materials: Envelopes with addresses of congregational members; blank cards to be used in making Christmas cards. (Cooperation of parents will be necessary.)

1. How many of you know what special day of the year will soon be here? Yes, Christmas is only a few weeks away. Do you like Christmas? Why? (Give just a brief time for the children to respond.)

2. What are some of the things you and your family do as you get ready for Christmas? What preparations do you make? (Younger children may have difficulty remembering. The older children can respond more adequately. In any event, you may give clues to various preparations. Many of the responses will not be of a "religious" nature. There is no need to force responses into that direction.)

3. Yes, those are many things that we do as Christmas approaches. In our family we do many of those things. One thing that we do in my family, and I am sure you do in your family, is send Christmas cards. (If a child earlier mentioned Christmas cards, refer back to it.) How many of you remember sending or receiving Christmas cards last year? Can you remember what any of them looked like? (Give opportunity for responses.)

4. Why do we send Christmas cards to each other? What do you think? (Give opportunity for responses. Responses may include: "It's nice." "It's fun." "To wish someone Merry Christmas." Acknowledge the responses.)

5. Let me tell you why I send Christmas cards. I send cards to people whom I will not see at Christmas. I want to say to each one of them: "I like you; I am thinking about you." I want to tell them again that Jesus is born and that God loves them.

6. In our family here at _____ some of our friends will not be able to worship with us during these next weeks and on Christmas. Many of them are ill and must stay at home. We sometimes call them shut-ins. Some of our friends live in homes for older people. So I would like for you to help me and our congregation to send a Christmas card to each of these friends who cannot worship with us.

7. I have some materials here for you. On each envelope is the name of a person for whom one of you will make a card. You make the card the way you wish. (Give each child an envelope already addressed. You may say something about the person to whom it is addressed.)

8. Work on your card this week. Bring it back here next week, and I will ask that you place it on the offering plate. (On the following Sunday, at a specific time, ask the children and parents to come and place the cards on the offering plates.)

Age suitability: Preschool (but only if parents are involved) and elementary.

A Choir of Angels

Aim: To assist children in doing what angels do—in speaking a message from God.
Material: Bible.

1. I want to read for you a story from the Bible, a story that tells of angels. (Read Luke 2:8–15.)

2. There were many things mentioned in the story, but it does talk of angels. What do you think an angel is? (Responses will be many and varied: long white robes, wings, ring around the head, invisible, no shoes, etc. Accept the responses as belonging to the children. Do not put values of "right" or "wrong" on the responses. The responses are not occasions for argument with the children. A verbal correction will not be useful nor helpful. Give new challenges and problems.)

3. What do you think angels do? (Responses may include: sing, live in heaven, fly around, etc. The responses belong to the children and should be honored as such.)

4. In our story, what did the angels do? (There may be the need to reread portions of the story. If a child mentions "good news," or "telling," focus on that item.) Yes, the angels told good news. They were bringing a message from God. They told about Jesus.

5. (If a child does not identify "good news" or "telling," you can use verbal pointers.) One thing that I noticed is that the angels told good news, told good things from God. They brought a message from God.

6. Do you now any angels? (Many will respond negatively. Others might name a parent, teacher, or the pastor.) Why do you think they are angels? (A child may respond, "My mommy sometimes calls me an angel." Your response could be, "Why do you think she calls you that?" or, "That's interesting. My mother called me an angel sometimes." Be prepared for the child who wants to tell you the "other names" used by his mother. You may get the response, "Charlie's Angels." "Yes, I see why you say that. There is a television program with that title.")

7. You know what? I have known some angels—men and women, boys and girls who have given me a message from God. Guess what I want you to be today. That's right, I want you to be a choir of angels.

Can you guess what I want you to do? (Give time for responses. To some of the suggestions you might respond, "That's interesting. But no, not right now.")

8. I want you to tell the other members of the congregation some good news. Let's all stand, facing the congregation, and let's tell them, "We love you. God loves you." (Repeat the two sentences for the children. Encourage the children to shout out the two sentences. Join with the children.) Thank you for being angels today.

Variations:

a) After the children have spoken to the congregation, have the congregation speak the same message to the children.

b) As the children return to their seats, they could be encouraged to stop with one or two people and say, "I love you. God loves you." Encourage the congregation to respond in like manner.

Age suitability: Preschool and elementary.

Happy Birthday, Jesus

Aims: To focus attention of the children on Jesus, who had birthdays as they do.

To help children to celebrate the birth of Jesus in ways familiar to them.

Materials: Sponge cake (no icing), candle for cake, knife, napkins; alert organist to play the hymn, "Away in a Manger"; colored paper streamers.

1. Christmas is almost here. Are you excited? What do you like about Christmas? (Many responses will focus on the children themselves, especially on the gifts they anticipate.) What are some of the special things that you, your family, and friends do during the Christmas season? (Responses will include Christmas trees, gifts, visits to Santa Claus, etc. You might assist them by making additional suggestions.) Yes, Christmas is a very happy and exciting time; I like it very much.

2. But why do we celebrate Christmas? (Give opportunity for the children to reply. Responses will be mixed. In all probability, at least one of the children will mention Jesus.) That's right, it's Jesus'

birthday. It is the date that we have chosen to celebrate the day that Jesus was born as a baby as you were. Do any of you remember the date of your birthday? (Give opportunity for those able to state their birthdates.) If you cannot remember right now, ask your parents when you return to your seats. Maybe you will want to tell me the date after the service today.

3. I have another question. How do you think that Mary and Joseph, Jesus' parents, might have celebrated his birthday? Take a guess. (The responses will reflect the experiences of the children at birthday parties—playing games, presents, cake and ice cream, singing "Happy Birthday," etc.) Are those some of the things that you have done at parties? They are all very good suggestions, but we really don't know how they may have celebrated Jesus' birthday.

4. Though we don't know how Mary and Joseph may have done, let's use some of your suggestions to celebrate Jesus' birthday. But first, let's thank God for the birth of Jesus, and for your birth. (You should include not only thanks for Jesus but for the children, mentioning them by name.) Look what I have here—a cake with a candle. (A child may want to describe another cake that he or she has seen.) But before we cut it and eat it, what should we do? Yes, blow out the candle and sing. Instead of singing "Happy Birthday" let's sing a hymn that we know, "Away in a Manger." (Sing just one verse with the children.) Now that we have sung one verse, let's ask our other friends in the congregation to join with us in singing.

5. (Following the hymn, share the cake with the children. If some is remaining the children may share with others in the congregation.) And look what else I have—some colored paper streamers. Rather than decorating the room, I will decorate you. And then I want you to decorate one or two people in the congregation. (Put streamers around the shoulders of the children, instructing them how to put the streamers on others. Give each child one or two streamers and send the children into the congregation. Remaining cake should be distributed at this time. Depending upon the number of children involved, it may not be desirable to do all the activities. In making a choice, include one that will give opportunity for interaction between the children and others in the congregation.)

Age suitability: Preschool and elementary.

Jesus the Light

Aim: To discuss the use of candles in worship and to point to Jesus as Light.

Materials: Candles for communion table or altar, other candles if desired, matches.

1. Maybe you noticed that these candles are not lighted, nor are they in their usual places. They are here (on a small table or even on floor) so that we can see them better. Let's talk about candles for a few moments. Do you and your family ever light candles in your home? Tell us some of the times when you light candles at home. (Responses: in the evening at a meal, when friends come, at Christmas, when the lights go out, etc. You can assist the children by asking, "Have you and your family lighted candles when . . .?")

2. Candles are beautiful. I like to watch the flame of a candle. The flame often looks as if it is dancing. Look at the flame of a candle sometimes and watch it dance. (If a child speaks of the dangers of "playing with fire" reinforce that concern.)

3. How many of you use candles to light up your homes? How many of you read by candlelight? (A child may want to relate a story of a person who read by candlelight.) No, very few of us use candles for reading or for lighting our homes. We have electricity with lamps and light bulbs. But what would happen—and maybe this has happened to you—if all the electricity in your home did not work during a storm? Has that ever happened at your home? What did your parents do? Did they light a candle?

4. What happened when you lighted that candle? (Give opportunity for response.) Yes, there was light in the room. It kept you from bumping into things. It showed you where to walk. You probably felt better having the light of just one candle.

5. In the Bible Jesus is called the Light of the world. Do you have any idea why the Bible calls Jesus the Light of the world? (This is an extremely difficult question for children. Responses may be trivial. Do not make "corrections" or offer information which is not useful to the children. You can do little more than give a "verbal pointer.")

Jesus is something like a light, something like that candle in the dark room. Jesus tells us who God is.

6. So when we put lighted candles in the sanctuary we don't put them there so that we can see better. They are there to tell us something; they tell us a story; they remind us that Jesus is the Light that shows us who God is. Now I will light the candles and place them in their usual place to remind us and our friends that Jesus is the Light that shows us who God is.

7. And now let's tell our friends the story that the candles tell. "Jesus is the Light that tells us who God is." (Practice the sentence with the children, and then have them tell the story.)

Age suitability: Primarily elementary. (Preschoolers will encounter difficulty with the highly verbal and relational elements in this strategy.)

Refreshing Water

Aim: To focus attention on water as the element used in baptism.
Materials: Large pan or pail of water; cloth for wiping hands.

1. See what I have here today. Just a large pan (pail) of water. Water can be fun and exciting; it is very important for our life. I like the feel of water as it moves over my fingers and drops off. Like this. (Dip your hands in the water; bring them out of the water, letting the water roll off.) Do you like the feel of water? Would you like the water to roll off your hands? (Invite children to dip their hands in the water and watch the water drip off. Wipe their hands.)

2. Let's talk about water for a few minutes. What are some of the ways we enjoy water or use water? (Responses may be many. Share the excitement of the children. Responses: swimming, bathing, drinking, washing clothes, seashore, etc.) Yes, you have mentioned some of the ways that we enjoy water.

3. When we are thirsty and have a drink of water, we feel good. We say sometimes that we are refreshed. When we are hot and have the opportunity to go swimming or have someone sprinkle us with a hose, we feel good. We are refreshed.

4. Water is very important. Water is needed so that we can have

food. One our our hymns in church reminds us that "God sends the soft, refreshing rains" to give water to plants, the fields, the gardens. We need water so that we can live. At one place in the Bible, Jesus is called "the living water." (Some of the older children may speak of the destruction brought by water. Accept their contribution, suggesting that we are always seeking for means to control the water.)

5. Water is very necessary for our lives. It is very important to us. Shortly, we will have a baptism. Do you remember what I will put on the baby's head? That's right, water. When you were baptized, water was put on your head. In baptism, when we speak our words and put water on the person, that person is a member of God's family in our congregation here. So we use water, a very important thing for life, when we baptize.

6. During the baptism, watch for the water. Stay here and you will be able to see better.

Age suitability: Preschool and elementary.

Stories Our Church Building Tells

Aims: To focus attention on the symbols of the faith located in the church building.

To hear the stories related to those symbols.

To assist the children to share their "picture-stories" with the congregation.

Materials: Secure the commitment of some adults who will assist the children in making banners and collages which are to be used as hangings on pulpit and altar.

1. There are many things here in our church building that tell us stories about God, about Jesus, and about persons and events in the church: Windows. Cross. Altar (or communion table). Pictures. Hangings on the altar (communion table) and the pulpit. The people who made these things want to tell us some stories. Each week as you come here you are able to see these things, these stories. Of all these, what do you like to look at the most? Which one interests you? (Give the children opportunity to make a choice, selecting two items which they like. Otherwise, they will continue to identify everything.)

2. Would you please share with us why you like that? (This may be a difficult question for some children. "It's pretty." "I like the colors." "I don't know; I just do." To push hard on the "Why?" may demand more than the child is able to produce. Affirm the children's attempts.) Yes, I see why you might choose that. Do you have any ideas of the story that it is telling us? (Some children, using their experience and the repertoire of religious language, may be able to tell a story. Give the children opportunity but do not force.)

3. I want to point out one of my favorite items and talk about the story it tells us. (Choose a window, a picture, a carved symbol, symbols on the communion table or altar, or pulpit hangings. Tell the story in simple language, avoiding complicated language. If at all possible, let the children touch the items about which you are talking.)

4. Did you like that story? Can you tell me something about the story you did like? (You are asking for responses to the story. Accept what is offered. You are discovering how a particular child puts information together. If a child says he or she did not like the story, accept that. Recognize verbally that we all do not like the same stories.)

5. Now for the next several weeks I want you to make something which tells a story about God or Jesus. I have asked your church school teachers to assist you in making hangings for the communion table (or altar) and pulpit. We will hang them in their places and you will have the opportunity to share your stories with the congregation. *Variation:* This strategy can be used on several occasions. There can be different age groupings. The adult assistants should help the children to make a paper collage or a banner. Give the children freedom. A "perfect" job is not the object. On succeeding Sundays, have the children's works hanging on the altar (communion table) or pulpit. Give opportunity for the children to talk about their picture-stories. Do not ask, "What does this mean?" or, "What is that?" Such questions tend to limit responses. Rather, invite the children, "Tell us about your picture-story." Different children may relate different stories. Give the children freedom.

Age suitability: Primarily kindergarten and elementary.

The Season of Lent

Aims: To introduce children to the word, "Lent."
To encourage family devotions.

Materials: Prepared materials for family devotions. (You can prepare a series of family devotions designed with a special concern for children, including a scripture verse, a hymn suggestion and a short prayer.) One devotion to be used with the children. Prepared family devotional material for the congregation.

1.   Each year is divided into four seasons. Do any of you know how we describe those four seasons, those four times of the year? (Younger children will have great difficulty with this question. They do not understand the use of the word "seasons." The elementary school children will be able to respond.)

2.   Can you tell me some of the things that you especially like to do during spring? summer? fall? winter? (Give the children opportunity to respond. Share in their enthusiasm related to their activities.)

3.   The church also divides the year into times and seasons. The church does special things in each season. Let me just name some for you. You may not recognize all, but you will recognize some. Some of the words may sound funny to you. Advent. Christmas. (How many of you know what that's about? Tell me.) Epiphany. Easter. (How many know what that's about? Tell me.)

4.   Right now we are in the season named "Lent." The church has always used this season for a special thing. Lent is a special time to read the Bible, and to say our prayers. These things we do all other times of the year. Lent calls us to make special efforts in reading the Bible, saying our prayers, and worshiping.

5.   One of the special things that we can do during Lent is to have family devotions if we do not already do them at home. I have prepared some family devotions that you and your family can do at home. Let's do one of them here. (Go through the devotion.)

6.   I will give each one of you this guide for family devotions. Ask your family to use these, perhaps at the evening meal, before bedtime, at breakfast, or at some other time.

7.   (If there are other prepared materials for adults, ask the

children to distribute them at that time or ask them to distribute them at the doors at the close of the service. In either event, give clear directions to the children.)

Variation: Throughout the season, even continuously, you could prepare additional material for family devotions with a special concern for the children. These would be distributed periodically to the children. On occasion, you could discuss with the children their use of the materials. But take care: some children may not have been given the opportunity for devotions at home.

Age suitability: Primarily elementary. (Preschoolers can participate in the events but will not understand the conversation related to seasons.)

Postures in Prayer

Aim: To assist the children to use both words and body in prayer.
Material: None.

1. Today I want to discuss the ways in which our bodies talk, the ways in which our bodies tell other people things about us. Have you ever thought about the ways that your body talks? (Give opportunity for responses. If a child says, "With my mouth," respond, "Yes, that's one way. Are there others?" Some may give appropriate descriptions of "body language." Remember those descriptions for later use.)

2. Let's try a few things. Show me what you do when you are excited. Show me how you stand when you are angry. How do you walk when you are in a hurry? Show me a sad face. Show me a happy face. (In each instance, give the children opportunity to react.)

3. Our bodies do "talk." Our bodies tell other people when we are happy, sad, angry, excited, or in a hurry.

4. During a worship service, do you ever watch people as they pray? What do we do with our bodies (our heads, our hands) during the prayers? (A child may suggest that we are to keep our eyes closed during prayer and not to look around. Accept the statement. There is no need to agree or disagree in any argumentative manner.) We do look around sometimes and that's all right. What are some of the things that people do with their bodies (hands and heads)? (Be alert

and careful, for a child may identify some "odd" behavior of a congregational member.)

5. There is no one thing that we must always do with our bodies (hands and heads) while we are praying. The many things that we can do all tell something; they all "talk."

6. (Involve the children in a series of body activities. You can ask them to suggest what the various types of "body language" tell others about our prayer. You can make interpretations of the activities. Closed eyes: thinking and concentrating on one thing, blocks out things that would distract us; standing: showing respect for a person; folded hands: showing reverence and honor; kneeling: honoring a king or a lord; hands outstretched with palms opened upward: expecting that God will bless us; prostration of the body on the floor: tells others that God is great; sitting: posture of conversation.)

7. We have done various things with our bodies (hands and heads) that we can do while praying. All those actions tell special messages. I will lead us in a prayer, and you do the actions that you wish. (Do not expect that all children will use the same actions. Give them freedom.) Perhaps when we pray at other times in church, you will want to use some of these actions.

Age suitability: Preschool and elementary.

Jesus Loves Me Even if I Have Done Bad Things

Aims: To help the children to talk about their feelings.

To speak a "good word" to the children.

To assist them in speaking a "good word" to others.

Material: None.

1. Today I have several very hard questions to ask you, but I am sure that you will help me. Do you ever do some things that you should not do? Have you ever done things that someone has called "bad"? (Give time for the children to respond. You are in an extremely sensitive area. Some children may be reluctant to respond

because of painful memories of punishment, both verbal and physical. You are in the area of parent-child relationships. By necessity of experience children will talk about their parents. Other children may be more free in talking than some parents might wish. Do not register surprise. Do not "argue" with the children about their feelings. Do not create embarrassment for parents. Move in a matter-of-fact way.)

2. So, would you share with me one or two things that you have done that you should not have done? (Responses may appear trivial and inconsequential to adults. Children have been told that certain things are "bad." What is minor to adults may be extremely important to children. If the children are reluctant, you may need to make some suggestions, perhaps drawing from your own childhood.)

3. Have you ever been punished for some of the things that you have done? (Some may want to describe the kind of punishment received. Don't dwell on those descriptions. Again, deal with these responses in a matter-of-fact way.)

4. How do you feel when you have done something that might be "bad," or when you have been punished? (Permit the children to struggle with the question. They may express intense emotions or verbal hostility. You have asked about their *feelings*. This is not the occasion to argue with their feelings or to suggest that they ought not to feel certain ways.)

5. Yes, quite often we do feel unhappy or badly or sad about some of the things that we do. And, yes, when we are punished we do feel angry or hurt or very much alone. Sometimes we don't understand. But even when you do bad things your parents love you. They love you even if you do bad things and even if they punish you. That is hard to understand sometimes. But they love you.

6. And there are others who always love us. You are my friends, and I love you. All of us are the friends of Jesus, and Jesus loves us even if we have done bad things.

7. Today I want you to help me with the sermon. I have something that I want you to say to all the other friends in the congregation. Let's practice those words. (Practice with the children, having them repeat, "Jesus loves you even if you have done bad things.") Let's stand at the pulpit where I usually stand for the sermon, and together let's speak this happy word to our friends.

Age suitability: Primarily elementary. (Preschoolers will encounter difficulty in verbal articulation. They will focus on very minute items which have been labeled "bad" by parents. They will focus also on punishment. They can, however, participate in speaking a word.)

Jesus and the Lepers

Aims: To provide the opportunity for children to react to a Bible story.

To provide the opportunity for prayer.

Material: Bible. (Luke 17:12–19. Read the story from the Bible, a modern translation.)

1. Today I want to read you a story from the Bible. When I am finished I want you to tell me what you think about the story. (You are not asking, "What is the story about?" Rather, "what do you think about the story?" Read the story slowly.)

2. First, are there any words in the story that you did not understand? (The word "leper" will cause difficulty for some. In any event, ask the children, "What is a 'leper'?" Responses may be odd, even funny. Affirm the children's attempts. There is no need to declare a response "wrong." You should add the appropriate information.) Leprosy is a disease which many people had in the land where Jesus lived. People were afraid of the disease. Those who had the disease were called "lepers." People did not like to be near lepers. They did not want to touch a leper. They were afraid they would catch the disease. Lepers, people who had the disease, had to live away from the people who did not have the disease. (If much time is devoted to the explanation, reread the story.)

3. What do you think about the story? Did you like it? Why? (Some may respond with a "Yes" and others with a "No." In each case, ask the children for more information.) Which person in the story do you like the most? the least? (In the conversation the children may focus on insignificant details of the story. They may not be able to make logical sense of the story. You have asked what they think and the character liked or disliked. Thus, do not "correct" the children.

Encourage them in their attempts.) Your responses are very interesting, and I am happy that you have shared them with us.

4. You have shared with me; I want to share with you my thinking and feeling. (Keep your language direct and simple. Do not attempt to impose complicated or abstract thinking on the children.) One example: There are two things I liked in the story. Even though people feared the lepers and made the lepers stay by themselves, Jesus cared about them, loved them, and wanted to help them. Jesus often helped persons whom other people did not like. Second, at least one of the men returned to thank Jesus. When others have helped us, it is important that we thank them. It is unforunate that the other nine forgot.

5. So before you return to your seats, let us pray, thanking God that he loves and cares for us and all people regardless of who they are. (Lead the children in a prayer. You might have them practice a prayer which they can say in unison.)

Age suitability: Preschool and elementary.

Hosanna in the Highest

Aim: To provide an opportunity for the children to participate in a Palm Sunday parade.

Materials: Bible (Matthew 21:1–9), parts of palm branches, balloons, colored paper streamers.

1. One day Jesus wanted to enter the city of Jerusalem in a special way. So he and his friends decided to have something of a parade. We don't know much about the parade, how big it was or how many people were there. I want to read to you from the Bible the story about that parade. This is Palm Sunday. The story is often called the Palm Sunday story.

2. (Read Matthew 21:1–9. Read the story without any discussion of its contents.)

3. What is something that you like about the story? (Give opportunity for responses.)

4. I want you to recall two items. First, some of the people in the parade had cut some branches, probably palm branches, and spread them on the street as Jesus rode the donkey. Second, some of the people shouted, "Hosanna to the son of David." "The son of David" is another name for Jesus.

5. Today I want us to have our Palm Sunday parade. It won't be exactly like the parade Jesus had, but it will be something like that parade. Here is part of a palm branch for each of you. And there are some balloons and paper streamers. I want us to parade in the aisles of the church and say to our friends, "Hosanna to the Son of David. Hosanna in the highest." (Practice the words with the children several times.)

6. I will lead you down the aisles. Let's wave our branches, balloons, and streamers. And let's proclaim our message to our friends.

Variation: With some rehearsal prior to the worship service the children could act out the story as it is being read. Children could be cast in the various roles. Such an approach would produce greater order but would diminish spontaneity.

Age suitability: Preschool and elementary. (The variation is more suitable for elementary.)

Jesus Lives

Aim: To provide children the opportunity to participate in the Easter proclamation.
Materials: Noisemakers, horns, bells, tambourines, banners, party hats, etc.

1. This is a very special day. How many of you know the name of this day? (Give opportunity for the children to respond. Most will identify the day.)

2. Yes, today is Easter. Why is this a special day? What do you do to celebrate this day? Has any special thing happened? (Most of the children will speak of Easter eggs, Easter baskets, candy, bunnies, or new clothes. Such responses reflect the experiences of the children, and the children should be given opportunity to talk about them. Even if a child should identify the Christian particularity of the day, do not abort the other conversation prematurely.)

3. Yes, all those things are interesting. This is also a very special day in our church. Can any of you suggest why this is a special day for our church? (Some of the older children may use the traditional formula, "Jesus rose from the dead." Others may be used. Receive the responses, but it is not wise to explore more deeply the formula. Comparisons between Good Friday and Easter are not helpful. "Resurrection" is an extremely difficult problem for children. Complicated explanations are of little value to the children. If a child does speak of "Jesus rose from the dead," your response should be simple and declarative: "Yes, Easter tells us that Jesus is alive. Jesus lives.")

4. Easter is a special day which tells us, "Jesus lives. Jesus loves and cares about us." I am happy and glad when I hear that news.

5. On special days we often have parades. People are excited; they are happy. And today I want us to have a parade here in church. I want us to parade in the aisles. I have brought a number of items that we can use in our parade. (Give an item to each child.) As we parade in the aisles ring the bells and use the horns. And we will shout out, "Jesus lives."

6. I have asked the organist to play one of the Easter hymn tunes for our parade. I will go with you in the parade. When I hold my hand up high, we will stop and shout out, "Jesus lives."

7. (While the children are still in the aisle, invite the congregation to share in the proclamation.) We have been parading and shouting. Let's ask our friends to join the shouting. Let's ask them to shout out, "Jesus lives. Praise be to God." (Lead the congregation. It may be desirable to repeat the proclamation two or three times.)

Age suitability: Preschool and elementary.

What Is the Church?

Aim: To assist the children in thinking of the church as people.
Materials: Sheets of drawing paper, one for each child; crayons, two or three for each child; board on which drawings can be displayed by use of masking tape.

1. (The first part of this event should be at the beginning of the worship service.) For a few minutes during the first part of the service I want you to do something like "homework." I have here some sheets of drawing paper and some crayons. I am giving you the word "church" and I want you to draw whatever you think "church" is. Then we will display the drawings and talk about them.

2. (Distribute the paper and crayons. The children could return to their seats. If possible, permit the children to remain in the front of the church, reminding them to work quietly.)

3. (After some time, gather the children again. Let each display his or her drawing.) Please tell us about your drawing. (Leave the invitation open. Do not ask "What is it?" The question forces a closure on the child's thinking. Concerning various items in the drawing, always ask, "Would you tell me about that?")

4. (Most of the drawings will be of buildings or of symbols in the worship area. If one should illustrate people, use it later in the conversation.) Thank you very much for the drawings. When we think of "church," we do think of our buildings—the windows, cross, steeples. (Mention items on the drawings. If a picture does illustrate people, add, "Ann's picture included something else. Can you look at the picture and tell?")

5. Yes, that's right. It is true that we do think of "church" as the building we worship in or where we go to church school. And the church is something else also. Do you have any suggestions about that "something else"? The church is people. The church is the family of God. Do you know where there is a family of God, of God's people? (Give opportunity for response. Some may suggest that the congregation is the people of God or that they are God's children.)

6. Yes, we are the family of God; we are God's children. And we are the friends of Jesus. You, all of our friends in the congregation,

and I—all of us are the church also. We can talk about the church as a building; but also the church is you, all of us here. We are God's family. Let's have our friends join with us as we speak a truth about ourselves. (Practice with the children, "We are God's family; we are the church." Have the entire congregation join in that statement.)

Variation: Children could be asked to draw what they think "God" is and then share their drawings. This request could be made in a church school class prior to the service. In such tasks, do not direct, "Draw what God looks like." Rather, "I am going to give you a word, and I want you to draw what you think _____ is."

Age suitability: Preschool and elementary. (The variation would be more suitable for elementary.)

How Big Is Your Family?

Aim: To focus the attention of the children on the congregation as a special family, a family of God.

Material: Banner of cloth or paper (suitable for a parade in the aisles) on which is written, "Brothers and sisters in the family of God."

1. Today I want us to talk about your special family at home and then about another special family. How many persons are in your family at home? (Give opportunity for the children to give numbers, perhaps naming a few family members. Preschoolers will be able to give names; they will have difficulty with numbers. Be sensitive to those children with divorced parents or from single-parent families. A child may want to tell of a divorced parent or one no longer living at home. In one instance, a child announced that his father was in prison. Do not be embarrassed by the responses. Accept and acknowledge statements.)

2. Can you think of other members of your family who do not live at your house? (Here, again, you may hear a concern for divorced parents, separated parents, or even a dead parent. Acknowledge but do not permit these to become the major thrust.) Grandparents? Aunts and uncles? Brothers and sisters?

3. Our families are very special to us. There are special things that

we do with our families: Help each other. Show love to each other. Have family get-togethers. Go on vacations.

4. How many brothers and sisters do you have? (Give opportunity for response. The children may want to name brothers and sisters.)

5. I want to tell you about some more brothers and sisters that you have. I want to tell you about another special family, God's family. Do you know where God's family lives? (This may be a difficult question for some children. Some may mention some cities. Others may say, "Up in heaven." Let them attempt responses.)

6. All of the people in the congregation—you and (*you can mention by name some of the members*) and I—all of us are God's family. And just think! We are brothers and sisters in the family of God. Isn't that amazing! All of the persons in the congregation are our brothers and sisters. We all belong to the family of God. We have a lot of brothers and sisters.

7. I have a banner here on which is written, "We are all brothers and sisters in the family of God." Let's walk in the aisles and call out, "We are all brothers and sisters in the family of God." (Practice with the children.) O.K., I will go with you.

8. Let's ask the congregation to say the same to us and to each other. (Enlist the congregation's cooperation.)

Age suitability: Preschool and early elementary.

What Do You Think of God?

Aim: To provide opportunity for the children to reflect upon and describe their understanding of God.
Material: None.

1. As we have been together each Sunday, I have asked you a lot of questions. Some have been easy; some have been hard. We have done many things together. We have talked about many things. In many of our conversations we have talked about God. So today I want you to do a very special thing for me and our friends in the congregation. I want you to tell us what you think about God. Who is God? What does God do? (The children will probably respond to "What does God do?") How would you describe God for us? I want to know what you think. Who would like to start? (You may call upon one of the children to get the conversation started.)

2. (It is impossible to describe the variety of directions that the conversation might take. The questions, as stated here, open a wide arena for the children's imagination and fantasy. To ask "What does God look like?" is to prejudice the child's answers. It focuses upon anthropomorphic descriptions. Though most children will probably go in that direction, do not use such a question to compel the child in an anthropomorphic direction.)

3. (The intent here is not to discover how well the children have learned certain information and religious language. Rather, it is to give freedom to the children's imagination and fantasy as they deal with the word "God." You are asking the children what they think. Responses should be accepted and appreciated as those belonging to the children. No response should be ridiculed. There will be a wide diversity of responses.)

4. (Attempts to "correct" the children will not be fruitful. However, there are ways to challenge the thinking of children which may give them new experiences which may, in turn, assist them to think in more adequate ways about problems. First, especially with the older children, encourage them with new questions: "Why do you think that?" "How is that?" "Can you tell me more about that?" Such questions assist a child to think about his or her own thinking.)

5. (Second, the children may get into conversations with each

other. They may agree or disagree with each other. You should not only permit this but encourage it. In such activity the children may encourage and correct each other.)

6. (Third, you should share something of your thinking with the children. Your sharing becomes new information and a new experience which can assist the children in further thinking. Clues based on the children's earlier remarks will assist you in developing comments.) I am glad that you have shared with us. I have enjoyed it very much. Before we finish, I would like to share with you some things that I understand. (Keep the language within the experience of the children.) We want to thank you very much for sharing.

Age suitability: Preschool and elementary.

You Are the Saints of God

Aim: To assist children in discovering that they are the saints of God.

Materials: Pictures depicting saints in the early church and throughout the church's history. Include some pictures of congregational members. A mirror.

1. (Use the hymn "For All the Saints" or another hymn which refers to saints. One of the biblical passages mentioning saints could be used.) In the hymn we just sang, it speaks of saints. Do you remember? (There may be the need to repeat several phrases.) You have probably heard the word "saint" many times. What is a saint? Who is a saint? (Possible responses: people who lived a long time ago; dead people; people that are good; special people. Acknowledge the children's contributions with a simple, "I see." There is no need to agree nor disagree.)

2. Do you know the names of any saints? (Give ample time for responses. Possible responses: St. Peter, St. Paul, St. John, etc. If a particularly odd response is given, ask, "Why do you say that?" Such a question encourages the child to reflect further upon the answer. The answer gives you greater understanding of the child's thinking. To the child's answer respond, "Oh, I see. I understand what you are saying." Your response acknowledges the child and the contribution made and can serve as encouragement for future participation.)

3. I want to show you pictures of saints. Here is one which shows how one painter thought St. Peter might have looked. (Show several more, making a comment about each. If pictures of congregational members are used, ask if the children recognize the persons.)

4. Do you know any other saints? (Many will give a negative response. Some may name some adult—perhaps a parent, grandparent, teacher, or the pastor. One might inform you that his neighbor has a big saint—a St. Bernard. "That's a big dog, isn't it? Right now let's talk about people.")

5. Well, I know a lot of saints. Can you guess who are some of the saints I know? (Give time for responses and acknowledge the

contributions.) Let me tell you. Your parents and all the people in the congregation today—they are some of the saints I know.

6. Do you know what a saint is? What makes somebody a saint? (Responses may be similar to those elicited earlier. One may be added: people who go to church.) Yes, some of those things were said earlier. Let me tell you something about saints. Saints are God's people. Saints are the family of God. And all the people sitting in the congregation are saints, for they are part of God's family.

7. There is another saint that we have not talked about, a saint that I know. I want you to look at this saint. I want each of you individually to come next to me and look. If you know who it is, don't tell anyone until everyone has had an opportunity to look. Don't forget, don't tell anyone. (Have each child look into the mirror, reminding them not to tell.)

8. If you know who you saw, raise your hand. At the count of three, tell me who it is. (The "me's" will win.)

9. That's right. You are a saint. You are part of God's family just as the people in the congregation. You belong to God's family. You are a saint.

Variation: Prepare name tags which have written on them "Saint." Use tags that stick to clothes and put one on each child. Along with the word "Saint" there could be a blank in which the child's name could be written. Also, the children could distribute small flyers throughout the congregation: We are members of God's family; we are the saints of God.

Age suitability: Preschool and elementary.

God Send You a Happy New Year

Aim: To involve the entire congregation in wishing God's blessing for a happy New Year.
Materials: A calendar, sliced apples, honey.

1. Well, Christmas Day is past. Did you have a good Christmas? Tell me about your Christmas. (Give the children opportunity to talk. They may become excited and enthusiastic, especially concerning gifts received. There can be some negative responses. A child may not have received a desired gift, or a family argument during the season may be remembered. You can make simple acknowledgment of such responses.) No, we don't always receive everything we want, and we are disappointed. But what gift did you receive that you like? Yes, sometimes when we are very busy, we do get very tired, and we do argue and that can be unpleasant.

2. Did you do anything special? Did you go on visits or did some people visit you? Tell me about that. (A child may describe a party or other events. You will need to judge how extensive those descriptions should be.)

3. Christmas is over, and another holiday is coming. Do you know what is the next holiday? That's right, the New Year. Do you know what a New Year is? (This can be a difficult question for some children, calling for an understanding of which they are not capable. Nevertheless, encourage them to make efforts.) That is a rather difficult question, isn't it? Let me help a bit. Here is a calendar which helps us to count days. The days are divided into months, and there are twelve months. January, February, March, April, May, June, July, August, September, October, November, and December. When we count off all the days (365) from January through December we say that we have gone through one year. We have just completed all the days in December, so on January 1 we begin counting a new year.

4. Can you think of ways that people celebrate the coming of the New Year? (Some children will be able to respond: football games, going to church, parties, etc.) Yes, those are some of the ways; there are some others. (You might add to the list. It may even be necessary that you produce the list.)

5. One group of people had an interesting way of celebrating the New Year, and I want us to do it here today. They would dip sliced apples into honey and say to each other, "May God send you a happy New Year," then eat the apple. So take a piece of apple, dip it into the honey and eat it. (Some children may not like honey. Those who have never tasted it may be reluctant. Take care.) And let's say to each other, "God bless you and send you a happy New Year."

6. Let's face our friends in the congregation and say to them, "God bless you and send you a happy New Year."

7. And let's ask all our friends in the congregation to stand and greet each other with these words, "God bless you and send you a happy New Year."

Variation: The strategy could be implemented at the end of the service. The children could stand at the exits with the apple and honey for other members of the congregation. Greetings could take place as others take the honey and apples. Some adult assistance may be necessary.

Age suitability: Preschool and early elementary.

The Things I Like

Aims: *To provide the children with the opportunity to share with others something that they enjoy.*
     To provide opportunity for prayer.
Materials: This event is like the familiar "show and tell." On the preceding Sunday invite the children to bring an item which they enjoy. Enlist the cooperation of the parents. A printed note could be useful. You should bring an item also. Have a table on which to place the items.

1. Last week I asked you to bring with you today some item that you like and enjoy. Some of you have brought items, and I have brought one also. I want you to tell us about what you have brought. Tell us what you do with it. Tell us what you like about it. As we talk about our objects we will be sharing with each other.

2. (Give each child the opportunity to talk about his or her item. The younger children may simply identify the object. The older children may add some details. Those children who did not bring an object will want to "get into the act." Permit them to tell you about an object at home. We can help them listen to each other. Do you remember what Mary liked about her _____?)

3. (You should talk about your item. Describe it and tell why you like and enjoy it.)

4. It is a very wonderful and beautiful world that God has given to us. There are so many beautiful things in the world for us to like and enjoy. You have shared some of your toys and books. There are other wonderful things—the sunshine, the rain, our friends, our parents, our brothers and sisters, trees and grass, our friends here in the congregation. In our conversation we have shared with each other. God shares with us his beautiful world.

5. Before you return to your seats, let us pray, thanking God for our world. (You should guide the children in the prayer, naming specific items.) Thank you for sharing with us.

Age suitability: Preschool and early elementary.

Food Jesus Ate

Aims: To focus upon Jesus as a boy.

To provide an experience in sharing.

To practice prayer.

Materials: Raisins, dates, figs, pomegranates, or other foods characteristic of the Middle East; small paper plates; cloth for wiping fingers.

1. Today let's talk about food. How many of you like to eat? What are some of the foods you like to eat most? What are your favorite foods? (Give each child an opportunity to respond. There may be spontaneous agreements with each other. To one child's favorite food another may respond, "I don't like that. It tastes awful.") Not all of us like the same foods and that's all right, but Susan is telling us about *her* favorite food. And many of us do like the same foods. (You might indicate your favorite food.)

2. What foods do you like to eat the least? (Give each child opportunity to respond. You might indicate your least favorite food. Recognize that we all have likes and dislikes.)

3. There are a lot of different foods. Have you ever noticed all the different foods when you go to the food market? Many of those foods come from far off places. (Select a food not produced in the immediate area. Indicate that the food is grown in another part of the country or world and must be sent to us.)

4. People in different parts of the world have different favorite foods. When Jesus was growing up as a boy he lived in Palestine, a place far away from here. And he probably had favorite foods also. What kind of foods do you think that Jesus might have eaten and liked? (Children will draw upon their experiences, and responses may be wide and varied: cookies, hamburgers, hot dogs, potato chips, etc.) Yes, I can imagine that Jesus might have liked those foods, but it is not likely that Jesus had those foods.

5. But I do have some foods like those that Jesus probably ate when he was a boy—raisins, dates, figs, pomegranates. Have you ever tasted these foods? Do you like them?

6. Before we taste the foods let's thank God for our food, for the

people who grow our food, and for those who prepare our food. (Encourage the children to produce short sentence prayers. One child may suggest a prayer that all can say together. You may need to give an "example.")

Variation: Have some of the foods arranged on small paper plates. Have the children share the foods with members of the congregation. (I want you to share these foods with some of the members of the congregation. Please take the plates and share the foods and tell our friends, "This is some food like Jesus ate.")

Age suitability: Preschool and elementary.

Greet One Another with a Kiss

Aim: To assist and encourage the children to participate in the Kiss of Peace.
Materials: None.

1. When friends and relatives come to visit in your home, how do you and your parents greet them? What are some of the things you do first when they arrive? (Responses will reflect the experiences of the children in their homes: loud talking, waving, handshaking, eating, hugging, kissing, etc. Families have particular and even peculiar ways of greeting relatives and visitors, so be prepared for the unusual and for responses that could embarrass parents if explored further.)

2. (If no child mentions "kissing," move to another question.) When Gramma or Grampa come to visit, how do you greet them? (A child may tell you that she has no Gramma or Grampa. "Yes, this is true for many of us. Our grandparents are no longer with us.") Yes, you often give them a big hug and kiss. (Be prepared for the child who says, "I don't like to kiss my Grampa." Acknowledge the statement, "Yes, sometimes that's how we feel." There is no value in pursuing the question, "Why?")

3. When we greet a person with a hug or kiss, what do you think we are telling them? What do we want them to know? (Provide time for responses. Some may suggest "being in love." Other may describe parents' behaviors.) We are telling them that we are glad to see them, that we like them.

4. In the land where Jesus lived, friends usually greeted each other with a kiss on the cheek, sometimes both cheeks. The kiss said, "You are my friend. I am glad to see you. I like you." (Some children may react with an "ugh!" indicting a dislike or uneasiness.) Yes, that is a rather unusual habit for us and sometimes we don't like it.

5. In the Bible there is a letter that a man named Paul wrote to some Christians who lived in the city of Rome. In that letter he said to them, "Greet one another with a holy kiss." Many Christians did greet each other with a kiss on the cheek. Sometimes it was called the Kiss of Peace. (If the congregation uses the "passing of the peace" in

any fashion, make reference to that usage as related to the Kiss of Peace.)

6. I think that the practice of Christians greeting each other with a kiss is a good one. I wish that we practiced it more. You are my Christian friends. I love you. I am glad to see you. And today, I want to greet you with a kiss. (Give each child a kiss on the cheek, calling the child by name and saying, "I am glad to see you. I love you. God loves you.")

7. Now I have greeted you with a kiss. We are Christian friends. Would you give each other a kiss on the cheek and say, "I like you. God loves you." (The children may have difficulty responding to this suggestion. Encouragement, not compulsion, should be given.)

8. Now I have greeted you with a kiss. All of the other people in the congregation are our Christian friends. As you return to your seats, I hope that you will stop with one or two persons, give them a hug or a kiss and say, "I like you. God loves you." (The congregation, and parents in particular, should be encouraged to do the same for the children. You could lead the children into the congregation and give the Kiss of Peace to several members. You would, thus, model for and encourage the children.)

Age suitability: Preschool and elementary.

Jesus Loves All People

Aim: To assist the children to discuss a biblical story as they are able.

Material: Bible (Luke 19:1–10).

1. Today I want to read a story about Jesus from the Bible. You may have heard the story before. It is about a man named Zacchaeus whom Jesus met one day. Have any of you heard the story of Zacchaeus before? (Give the children the opportunity to respond "Yes" or "No." Do not have a discussion of the story at this point.)

2. After I have read the story I want us to talk about it, about what you like or do not like about the story, and the person in the story that you like the most. But before I read the story, let me tell you one thing about Zacchaeus. There were many people who did not like

Zacchaeus at all. They thought of Zacchaeus as a very bad man. (If a child asked why they did not like Zacchaeus, it will not be helpful to talk of the place of tax collectors in ancient Palestine. Rather, say that many believe Zacchaeus was dishonest, that he had taken money from others.)

3. (Read the story.)

4. Please tell me what you liked about the story? What did you not like about the story? (Encourage the children to talk about the story. Whatever they respond, accept it. You can probe with "Can you tell me more?" or "Why do you think that?" If they cannot respond further, move on.) What person or persons did you like most in the story? Can you tell us what you liked? (Again, accept the contributions of the children. Mere information given in an attempt to "correct" the children will not be adequate. Probes will both assist the children in their thinking and will give you clues to their understanding.)

5. (It is impossible to predict the directions in which children will travel with such a strategy. You may need to direct their attention to various items: Zacchaeus wanting to see Jesus and climbing the tree; Jesus inviting himself to Zacchaeus' house; people angry that Jesus would visit this man; Zacchaeus willing to repay anyone from whom he had taken money. It is not necessary to cover every item. Give the children the freedom to move as they are able.)

6. (At an opportune time, interrupt the conversation.) You have told us a lot of things that you think about the story. They have been very interesting, and I have enjoyed hearing you. I want to share with you something of what I think and feel about the story. (You can give verbal pointers to the children, such as the following.) I like Zacchaeus. He was willing to learn what he should do. And I like what Jesus did. It is not always easy to love all people. Even though many did not like Zacchaeus, Jesus loved him and cared about him. Jesus loved all kinds of people.

7. Let's end with a prayer. (You lead the children.) God, we thank you that Jesus loves us and all people. Help us to learn to love all people.

Age suitability: Preschool and elementary.

I Am a Disciple of Jesus

Aim: To assist the children in using the word "disciple" to identify themselves.

Materials: Name tags with the sentence, "I am _____, a disciple of Jesus"; felt pens to write in the name of each child.

1. I want to read to you a list of names and then talk about those names. Simon Peter. Andrew. James, the son of Zebedee. John. Philip. Bartholomew. Thomas. Matthew. James, the son of Alphaeus. Thaddeus. Simon. Judas Iscariot. (During the conversation with the children, it may be desirable to repeat the list.)

2. Do you recognize any of these names? (Some of the children may recognize their own names. You might indicate to a child that his name is on the list.) Do you know someone who has one of these names—a friend or a relative? (Give time for responses.) Yes, some of those names are very familiar to us. (A child may suggest that some of the names are funny. "Yes, they are funny because we do not hear them very often.")

3. The list of names that I read is a very special list of names. (A repeating of the list may be helpful.) Do any of you have any idea why this list is so special? (If a child has already indicated something about "disciples" refer back to that response.)

4. This list comes from the Bible and it has the names of the first twelve disciples of Jesus. What do you think a "disciple" is? (There may be a number of attempts to respond. If responses are strange or even wrong, there is no need to correct at this point. If a child responds a "friend" or "follower" of Jesus, pick up on that clue.) A disciple of Jesus is one who is a friend of Jesus, a follower of Jesus, and one who learns about Jesus.

5. Do you know any friends of Jesus? (The children may indicate parents, teachers, or even themselves. If names are given, pursue with the question, "Why do you think that?" And if a child indicates himself or herself, use that clue.) Yes, you—and you and you—and our friends in the congregation are disciples of Jesus. We are the friends of Jesus; we are learning of Jesus here in church, church school, and home; we are the followers of Jesus.

6. I have for each of you a name tag that you can stick on your

clothes. It is not just a name tag, but a special one for you. We will write your name in the blank. And when we have done that it will read "I am John (or Mary or . . .), a disciple of Jesus." I want you to wear this name tag, and others will know that you are disciples of Jesus.

Variation: Have a number of name tags with the sentence, "I am a disciple of Jesus." The children could distribute these throughout the congregation. Adults should be encouraged to wear the tags.

Age suitability: Preschool and elementary. (Preschoolers will not be able to deal adequately with some of the verbal content but can share in the "identifications" made and the name tags.)

Tell Me About Jesus

Aim: To provide opportunity for the children to describe and reflect upon their understanding of Jesus.

Material: None.

1. As we have been together each Sunday, I have asked you a lot of questions. Some have been easy; some have been hard. We have talked about many things. In our conversations we have talked about Jesus. So today I want you to do a very special thing for me and our friends in the congregation. I want you to tell us what you think about Jesus. Who is Jesus? How would you describe Jesus? I want to know what you think. Who would like to start? (You may need to ask one of the children to start.)

2. (It is impossible to predict the variety of directions that the conversation might take. The questions, as stated here, open a wide arena for the children's imagination and fantasy. It is not desirable to compel the conversation in one direction.)

3. (The intent here is not to discover how well the children have learned certain information and religious language. Rather, give freedom to imagination, fantasy, and conversation. You are asking the children what they think. Accept and appreciate responses as belonging to the children. No response should be ridiculed.)

4. (Responses will vary greatly. Some will look at Jesus as a miracle worker or a magician. Others will talk of him as a kind person. Still

other will speak of Jesus in the traditional religious language, such as: Savior, died on the cross, or dies for our sins. Remember that there is a wide gap between the use of that language and an understanding of its intent. One six-year-old asked, "Everybody is always talking about this guy Jesus coming again. When is he going to come here?")

5. (Attempts to "correct" the children verbally will not be helpful. You can challenge the thinking of the children and thus assist them to more adequate understandings. Especially with the older children, encourage them with new questions: "Why do you think that?" "How is that?" "Can you tell me more?")

6. (The children may get into conversation with each other. They may agree or disagree with each other. Not only permit this but encourage it. In such activity the children may encourage and correct each other.)

7. I am glad that you have shared with us. We have enjoyed it very much. Before we finish I would like to share with you some things that I understand about Jesus. (Your sharing becomes new information and a new experience which can assist the children in further thinking. Use language within the experience of the children and focus on the activities of Jesus and his dealings with persons.) Thank you very much for sharing with us.

Age suitability: Elementary. (The strategy is highly verbal and thus will create some difficulty for preschoolers.)

Welcome To Our Family

Aim: To provide the opportunity for children to greet new adult members.

Material: None.

1. From time to time we greet new members into our families. With the birth of a new brother and sister, we greet a new member into our families. (A child may offer the information that his family is expecting a new baby. Share in the anticipation of the event.) When one of our relatives gets married, we greet a new member into our family. (A child may indicate that she has gotten "a new Daddy" or "a new Mommy." Accept the information but do not probe.)

79

2. All of us here in our congregation (*name the congregation*) are a part of the family of God. You, our friends worshiping today, and I—all of us are a part of God's family. From time to time we greet new members into our family of (*name of congregation*).

3. There are some persons who have been visiting with us. They have said that they want to be members of our family here. You may even know some of them. In a moment we are going to have a brief celebration as they join our family. I want you to remain here.

4. After the celebration is completed I want you to greet and welcome these persons. I want you to shake their hands and you can give them a hug or a kiss if you wish and say, "Welcome to our family here at (*name of congregation*). (Practice the sentence with the children.)

5. (After the brief service, introduce the new members by name to the children. Do the same with the children. However, the number of persons involved may make this inadvisable.) I want you to be the first to greet these new members of our family. (Repeat the direction. Some children may be hesitant at first. You may need to walk along with them.)

Variations:

a) The child can be involved frequently in greeting new members. If the strategy is used frequently, the beginning point would be #2 above.

b) If children are among the new members, the children of the congregation could introduce them to the congregation.

c) Mimeographed sheets bearing the names of new members could be distributed to the congregation by the children.

d) Each child may introduce one of the new members to another person in the congregation.

Age suitability: Preschool and elementary.

A New Brother or Sister

Aim: To assist the children to greet a new brother or sister into the family of God.

Material: None (occasion: infant baptism).

1. Do you know what baptism is? Do you remember what we do in a baptism? (Give children opportunity to respond. Most of the

responses will focus on the activity involved in baptism, especially on water put on the baby's head. It is not useful to go into a theological explanation of baptism.)

2. Yes, one of the things that we do is to put water on the baby. Water is very important for baptism. Do you remember when you were baptized? (Most children will respond negatively. Be on the alert for the child who has not been baptized and who knows that fact.)

3. I don't remember either when I was baptized. My parents told me that I was baptized; I have a certificate, a piece of paper, which tells me when and where I was baptized. (You should show the certificate to the children.) You may have a similar certificate at home. Ask your parents to show it to you.

4. Not many of us remember when we were baptized. But whenever it was the minister put water on our heads. We became members of the family of God. In God's family I am your brother (or sister); you are my brothers and sisters. How about that! I am your brother (or sister). What do you think about that? (Give opportunity for response. The children may be surprised and even confused. They may indicate that you do not live at their homes. There may be other comments. You may need to talk of the special family at home and of the congregation as a special family of God.) We do certain things with our special family at home; we do certain things with our special family, the congregation.

5. In just a moment we are going to baptize _____. You stay here and watch the baptism. After that I have something that I want you to do.

6. (After the baptism.) I am going to take _____ into the congregation, and I want you to go with me. I want us to announce to the congregation, "This is _____, our new brother (or sister) in the family of God." (Take the newly baptized infant and walk in the aisles. Have the children make the announcement several times.)

Variations:

a) Show some of the children (all, if possible) their names in the church record book.

b) Ask if the baby knows about Jesus. How will the baby learn about Jesus? Many people will tell the baby about Jesus. The children can make a promise to help teach the baby. (Have the children sing a short hymn or song.)

c) After #4 above, there could be a celebration of the children's baptism. Special candles could be used. Dates of the children's baptisms could be announced. The first verse of "Children of the Heavenly Father" could be used as a celebration hymn.

Age suitability: Preschool and elementary.

I Am Special

Aims: To assist the children in thinking of themselves as similar to each other, yet each one being special.

To provide opportunity for prayer.

Materials: Pennies, one for each child. They should have distinguishing marks: different dates, shiny, dull, well worn, etc. (Other objects could be used.) Name tags: "I am _____. I am special." Felt pen.

1. How do I know that you are you and not someone else? John, if I were to say that you are Bob, what would you say to me? (Most often the children will identify themselves by their names. Or their parents. Or the house they live in.)

2. I have some pennies here. I will give one to each of you. Are these pennies all alike? Look at someone else's penny. Is yours exactly like that one? (Give time for the examination of the pennies.) Can you see any differences? (Direct the children to look for the distinguishing marks: dates, dullness, etc.) The pennies all have the same value. All of them are very similar to each other. Yet we can see some differences.

3. We are somewhat like the pennies. We are very similar to each other. We are all human beings. We all are valuable. No one is more important than another. We all have a nose, ears, fingers, toes, and hair. To let us know how important we are, the Bible tell us that God even numbers the hairs on our heads.

4. But can you tell me how you are different from other persons? Susan, can you tell me how you are different from Ruth? (Responses will focus on physical characteristics and activities. Such responses are within their experience and thinking abilities. It is not possible for the children to discuss qualitative differences. Thus, you will work with concrete elements.)

5. I have a nose. (Touch your nose.) You have a nose. Is your nose exactly like mine? No, your nose is special for you. I have ears. (Touch your ears.) You have ears. Are your ears exactly like mine? No, your ears are special for you. (Other parts of the body may be used.)

6. We are all very similar. We all look very much alike. Yet, each one of us is different from the other. Each one of us is special. The Bible tells us that God made everything special. You are special and God loves you.

7. I have some tags here. I will write your name on a tag and I want you to wear it. It reads, "I am (*John, etc*.) and I am special." You may keep the pennies. You may wish to place them in the offering plates as your offering today.

Variation: A variation could focus on the children's names. Bring some books with your name in them. Without opening the books ask, "Whose books are these?" Children may respond, "Yours." "But how would you know for sure? One way to tell would be to look for my name written in the book." The thrust of the variation would state that our names are important. Our names are our special names—even if others have the same name. Our names tell much about us. For one thing, they tell others about who our parents are.

Age suitability: Preschool and elementary.

You Are a Child of God

Aim: To assist the children in declaring another to be a child of God.

Materials: Name tags (self-sticking) with the sentence, "I am a child of God."

1. I am going to ask a rather strange question. Who are you? (Invite each child in turn to respond. This is an extremely difficult question for many children. Most will use their names in answering the question. Older children may offer additional descriptions.)

2. (Address each child in succession.) How do I know that you are _____? And that you are _____? (For the young children this is a difficult question. They have difficulty in understanding that a name is something given.)

3. When you were a newborn baby, you had no name. Your

parents gave you a name. That's who you are now. When you tell me or anyone else, you have told me something about you. You have told me who you are. Your name which your parents gave you is very important to you.

4. I want to tell you something else that I know about you. God loves you; you are a member of God's family here at _____. You are a child of God. Did you know that? What do you think about that? (Many children may have difficulty responding to the question. More important is the declaration that you have made. A young child, however, may be disturbed by the declaration. "Do I have to leave my Mommy and Daddy and go live with God?") We have parents who love us and care for us. We live in our special family. Also, you, all our friends here, and I, we are all God's children.

5. Now I want you to tell each other, "You are a child of God," and I want you to place a name tag on another person. It says, "I am a child of God." (Group the children in pairs. If there is an odd number, you work with one of the children. Instruct them to speak to each other and give help with the name tag if necessary.)

6. Now let's tell our friends in the congregation who they are. (Instruct the children to say to the congregation, "I am a child of God. You are a child of God.")

7. (Ask the congregation to respond in like manner to the children.)
Variation: If an additional supply of name tags is available, the children can distribute them to members of the congregation.
Age suitability: Preschool and early elementary.

Sometimes I'm Happy; Sometimes I'm Sad

Aims: To assist the children to talk about their feelings and to share in the feelings of another.

To assist them in speaking a "good" word to others.
Material: None (see the second variation).

1. Today I want us to talk about some of our feelings. All people are happy and glad sometimes; they are sad and angry at other

times. That is true of me. I am sure that the same is true of you.

2. So today, I want you to share with us some of the things that make you happy and glad and some that make you sad and angry. But first tell me some of the things that make you happy and glad, some things that you really like to do. (Give the children opportunity to talk. Share their excitement and enthusiasm.) Yes, those are very happy and glad things. I know you enjoy them very much.

3. You have told me some things that make you happy. Would you share with us some of the things that make you sad or angry? (Many of the responses will focus on family life. Children may reveal "family secrets." Do not prolong a discussion on those items. It is sufficient that the children have spoken and that you have listened. Children may reveal conflicts with parents. Now is not the time to resolve conflicts. If responses focus greatly on parents or the family, some acknowledgment should be given.) Yes, sometimes things which happen in our families do cause us to be sad or angry. Sometimes we do have difficulty with our parents, brothers, and sisters. That has happened to me many times. But you know, even at those times, our parents love us. (With reference to other responses, be accepting of the children's expressed feelings.) Yes, I can understand how those things might cause you to be sad or angry.

4. You have shared with me things about you. I want to tell you some things about me—times when I am happy and glad, times when I am sad and angry. (Relate one or two examples, keeping them within the children's experiences.) But I want to tell you something more, something I want to share with you, something that always makes me glad. Whether I am happy or sad, God loves me. Whether you are happy or sad, God loves you. Those are happy words for me. They are happy words that I want to share with you.

5. You know that I am a pastor. Each Sunday I talk with you and all our friends in the sermon. In the sermon I want to speak words that God wants us to hear. Today, I want you to help me in a part of the sermon. I want you to speak some happy words to our friends. (Indicate that they are to say, "Whether you are happy or sad, God loves you." Have the children practice the sentence.)

6. Let's gather around the pulpit where I usually stand when I preach the sermon. Together let us speak out happy, good words. *Variations:*

a) When discussing your role as the preacher, if the group

is not too large, invite each child to stand in the pulpit, giving the opportunity to see the congregation.

b) On a number of name tags (those that stick to clothing) have written "God loves me." Ask the children to distribute the tags to members of the congregation, encouraging the adults to put the tags on themselves.

Age suitability: Preschool and elementary.

Let's Celebrate

Aims: To declare to the children, "Jesus lives."

To assist children to participate in a celebrative event.

Materials: Balloons (use felt-tip pens and write on them "Jesus lives"); some stick signs with the same sentence (to be used by the older children); colored paper streamers.

1. How many of you have heard the words "celebrate" and "celebration"? (For some of the younger children the two words may cause some difficulty, resulting from the lack of familiarity with the words. You may need to give additional clues.) Do you recall some celebrations that you have attended? (Give opportunity for responses. Let the children make their attempts.)

2. What are some of the things that you and your family do to celebrate special occasions? Birthdays are special occasions. How do you celebrate birthdays? (Coke and ice cream, singing, games, etc. The responses will reflect the experiences of the children.) Have you ever been to a wedding? That was a special occasion. How did you celebrate that? (With all questions, give opportunity for the children to respond: singing, loud talking, dancing, eating, dressing up, and even a lot of drinking.)

3. Have you ever been to a parade? Which ones? Those were celebrations; those were special days. What do you remember of the parades? (Clowns, floats, noise, peanuts. If the children do not remember, you will need to give clues. Use local experiences and events.)

4. Have you ever been to any celebrations here in the church?

(The children may respond: a wedding, Easter, Christmas, a dinner, etc. Affirm responses given. If they give no responses, move on.)

5. Each Sunday morning that we worship here is a celebration. Can you think of anything that we do on Sunday morning which reminds you of a celebration? (Responses may be varied: sing; dress up; the pastor puts on different clothes; flowers. Some may recognize the processional as similar to a parade. You may need to give clues.)

6. Today I want us to have a celebration, and I want us to celebrate something special. Do you have any idea what that special thing may be? (If a child mentions Jesus in some manner, focus on that. If the children are unable to make responses, move on.) There is something very special about our worship: "Jesus lives and Jesus is our friend." When we worship, we are celebrating that Jesus lives.

7. So I want us to celebrate, and we will have a parade with balloons and signs and colored streamers. On the balloons is written, "Jesus lives." The same is on the signs. I want you to parade up and down the aisle, and along the way speak to our friends and say, "Jesus lives." (Let the children practice the sentence. Give some of them balloons, others signs; put streamers around the children's shoulders; let some children carry streamers. Have the organist play a hymn tune for the "parade.")

Age suitability: Preschool and elementary.

Workers in the Church

Aim: To enable the children to share in a task belonging to the worshiping community.

Materials: A box with a number of different tools. (Make arrangements with persons receiving the offering.)

1. Look at this. What do I have here? Right! Some tools. What do we do with tools? (Give opportunity for responses.) Yes, tools help us to do jobs. What are some of the jobs? What are some of the things that these tools help us to do? (Give the children opportunity to identify the tools and let them discuss the jobs which the various tools can do. If there are tools unfamiliar to the children, identify the tools

and even demonstrate, if possible. Some children may want to tell of other tools that are at home.)

2. Suppose I wanted to build a dog house, which tools would I use? Why? (Let the children discuss.) Yes, those are important tools which would help me build a dog house.

3. In some ways people, you and I, are like tools. We do certain jobs, and we help others get things done. Do you have any particular job at home? Is there a thing that you are supposed to do each day? Do you help your parents? (Give the children an opportunity to respond.)

4. When we are doing jobs we are called workers. Throughout the world God has a lot of workers. Can you name some? (Responses may be limited. You may need to identify some workers. There is no need to continue long on this issue.) Right here in our church, in our worship service, there are a number of workers, persons who do certain jobs. Can you name some? (Give opportunity for response. Again you may need to make suggestions. Organist, choir, pastor, ushers, janitor.) Yes, we need a number of people to do jobs for our worship service.

5. Today I want you to help in one of the jobs of our worship service. One of the tasks that the ushers do is to receive the offering each Sunday. I want you to help them. They will show you what to do. (The children and ushers should be together in the job. Also, let the children bring the offering forward with the ushers.)

Variation: If there is a special piece of literature for the congregation, let the children distribute it. (Note: Whenever we speak to the children about being helpers or workers of Jesus, it is important that we engage them in some task. The verbal announcement that they are helpers or workers is not very powerful. As we couple the verbal with an action behavior, we enable the children "to do as workers.")

Age suitability: Preschool and elementary.

Flowers: Our Offering

Aims: To provide the opportunity for children to make an offering to the worship service.

To provide the opportunity for sharing.

Materials: Flowers. (On the previous Sunday ask the children to bring flowers as a part of their offering to the worship service. Enlist the cooperation of parents. Perhaps a printed note will help. Have additional flowers for those who forget.) Vases with water; paper towels to wipe off flower stems.

1. (The first part of this event is at the beginning of the worship service, *not* before. Have several vases with water sitting on the floor.) Last week I asked you to bring some flowers today, and many of you have. I have some to share with you who do not have any. (Distribute flowers to the children.)

2. Each Sunday we have flowers in the church. They help to make our church beautiful. Today we are going to arrange the flowers in the vases in the sanctuary. This will be a part of our offering to our congregation and to God. They will help make our church beautiful; all of us can enjoy their beauty.

3. (Instruct the children to place the flowers in the vases. Do not be concerned about the arrangements. Assist the children in placing the vases of flowers in several locations. The children might select locations. Invite children who arrive late to bring their flowers. Leave a vase on the floor so that latecomers will have easy access.)

4. We will enjoy the flowers throughout the service. We thank you very much for your offering. At the end of the worship service I will ask you to come back here. I will give each of you some of the flowers. You will go to one of the doors and give a flower to each of our friends as they leave.

5. (Near the end of the service again call the children to the chancel.) As you share your flowers, say to our friends, "God loves you." And perhaps our friends will say to you, "God loves you." (Distribute flowers to the children. Indicate to them the exits to which they should go. Use paper towels to absorb some of the water.)

Variation: This strategy could be used several times throughout the spring and summer. Different groups of children could participate at different times.

Age suitability: Preschool and elementary.

Let's Dance

Aims: To experience body movements in relation to hymn tunes.
To suggest that our bodies are involved in our worship.
Materials: Arrange with organist to play three hymn tunes. The first should be lively, perhaps a march tempo. The second should be less lively, but suggest flowing movements. The third should be quiet and slow.

1. When you are home listening to the radio or watching television, do you ever dance to the music? Do you move your body with the music? How many of you do that sometimes? Do you like to do that? Why do you like to do that? Why is it fun? (The most usual responses may be: "It's fun" or "It feels good" or "I just like to." One might respond, "It makes my body happy.")

2. When the music gets loud and fast, what does your body do? (Give opportunity for responses: "Run." "Jump." "Hop.") Yes, you want to move faster and faster. When the music gets slow and soft, what does your body do? (Give opportunity for responses: "Walk slowly." "Tip-toe." "Crawl.") Yes, you want to move more quietly and slowly. Not only do our ears listen to the music, but our bodies also. Our bodies help us to enjoy the music.

3. Have you ever seen anyone dance in church? (Most responses will be, "No." Some may say that we are to be still and quiet in church.) Yes, often it is usual for us to be quiet and still in church. But I have seen people dance in church. And in the Bible there are some stories of people dancing in worship services. The way they moved their bodies told if they were glad or happy or sad.

4. When we sing hymns in the church, do you ever move your body with the music? Do you ever want to tap your feet or fingers? Well, in a way, that's dancing. Perhaps, we should move our bodies more when we sing our hymns.

5. I have asked our organist to play three hymn tunes today. As the tunes are played, I want you to move your bodies as you wish. (Select the slow, quiet tune as the last. At the end of each tune, comment on the children's movements. Indicate movements that you liked. Encourage the children.) It is fun to move our bodies; our hymns do

help us move our bodies in various ways. How we move our bodies does tell if we are happy or excited. Perhaps each Sunday as we sing our hymns you might move your bodies a little more than you usually do.

6. Before you return to your seats let's have a prayer, thanking God for our bodies which help us to enjoy so many things in our world. (You can lead the children in prayer or give them a "formula" that each may use. You might prepare a short prayer to be said in unison after practice.)

Variation: A person with some training in dance could demonstrate for the children. The children, for a time, will be observers. However, when the children are dancing, the model becomes an observer. It is not necessary that all the children make the same movements. The model will give clues and encouragement.

Age suitability: Preschool and early elementary.

Special Hymns

Aim: To provide the children an opportunity to work with and react to a portion of scripture, selected psalms, as they are able.

Materials: Bible. (Suggested psalms for usage: 8, 24, 46, 67, 95:1–7, 100, and 150. Use only portions of each.)

1. (The intent here is not to instruct the children about each part of the psalm's words. Rather, let the psalm remain poetry which may serve to stimulate the thinking and feeling of the children. Let them talk about their reactions to the psalm. You should share with the children what you find interesting and exciting about the psalm.)

2. In the Bible there is a section which is called "The Psalms." The psalms are hymns or songs that the Hebrew people sang in their worship services. In our worship services we often use the psalms, speaking them and singing them.

3. Today I want to read for you one of the psalms. Perhaps our friends in the congregation would like to follow along as I read. (Indicate the location of the psalm in the service book or the Bible located in the pew rack.)

4. (After reading the psalm slowly and carefully, we can ask a

number of questions which may stimulate the children's thinking and imagination.) What part of this psalm did you like? What did you think about as I read the psalm? Did any "pictures" come into your head? Were there some words that were difficult to understand? (If some difficult words are identified, invite other children to discuss those words. You may need to share your understanding.) What do you think this psalm is telling us? (It may be desirable to reread the psalm.)

5. What you have said has been very interesting. I want to share with you what is interesting and exciting for me in this psalm. (It is not useful to attempt an explanation or description of every part or word of the psalm. Select just one or two items to share.)

6. In the psalm there is one sentence which I would like us to learn. When we have learned it, we will invite the whole congregation to say it with us. (Examples of verses to be learned: Psalm 8:1; 24:1; 46:1; 67:3; 95:1; 100:5; and 150:6. Practice with the children.)

7. Now that we have learned a part of the psalm, let's use it in our worship here. (Invite the entire congregation to say the sentence.)
Age suitability: Primarily elementary. (Preschoolers will encounter difficulty in some of the tasks required.)

Let Us Pray with Words and Body

Aim: To assist children in the practice of prayer with both words and body.
Material: None.

1. When we are praying in church what are some of the things that we usually do? What are some of the things we usually do when we say our prayers? (Responses: bow our heads; fold our hands; kneel; say words; talk to God. For some children, the question may be difficult. Some of the body movements just mentioned may not have attracted the attention of the children. You may need to assist the children with, "Have you noticed that some people bow their heads or fold their hands?" If the children are able to respond, give them the opportunity. Do not insist that all people must bow heads or fold hands or kneel so as to pray rightly.)

2. When we pray we talk with both words and our bodies. Bowing our heads or folding our hands or kneeling are ways of talking with our bodies. Today I want us to take the Lord's Prayer and make some movements with our bodies as prayer. We will need to practice. (Speak the words slowly as the movements are explained and demonstrated. Having your back to the children as you demonstrate will make it easier for the children to imitate your movements.)

3. "Our Father, who art in heaven, hallowed be thy name." (Arms stretched upward—about a 45° angle with palms open and upward.)

4. "Thy kingdom come; thy will be done on earth, as it is in heaven." (Arms down—extended from the body somewhat with palms open and forward.)

5. "Give us this day our daily bread; and forgive us our trespasses as we forgive those who trespass against us." (Arms stretched forward from the body with palms open and upward.)

6. "For thine is the kingdom and the power and the glory, forever and ever. Amen." (Arms return to the first posture.)

7. (Practice several times with the children. You should demonstrate. It would be most desirable to ask the entire congregation to participate with the children. At the point of the Lord's Prayer in the service, speak the words slowly as the movements are executed. Participate with the children. Encourage the entire congregation to participate in the movements. Suggest to the children that they use the movements each Sunday. Other movements, more refined and detailed, could be added in the future.)

Age suitability: Preschool and elementary.

Our Beautiful World

Aims: To provide for the children experiences with the creation.
To assist children in acknowledging the creation as a gift of God.
To give the experience of prayer and sharing.

Materials: A nature table with items of the season. (Spring: small branch of tree beginning to bud, some garden seeds, green moss, some blades of grass, small box of dirt, even a jar with earthworms, a bunch of flowers, etc.)

1. Our world is so big. Our world is full of beautiful things. God has given us a wonderful world. All of you close your eyes for a few moments. Think of the things you like to look at, the things that you think are beautiful. Keep your eyes closed. I want you to tell me one thing that you think is beautiful. Raise your hands and I will call on you. (Give each child an opportunity to respond.)

2. You may open your eyes. (Continue in the following manner, "John, you said your dog. Can you tell me why your dog is beautiful to you?" This can be a very difficult question, especially for younger children. The responses may include " 'Cause" or "I just like it" or "It's red." Affirm their choices and give opportunity for the children to talk about those choices.) It is a wonderful world. In the world God gives, there are many beautiful things. (A child may want to tell of something he or she thinks is ugly. Permit the expression.)

3. We are in the springtime of the year, and there are so many beautiful things. Flowers are beginning to bloom; trees are getting new leaves; the grass is getting green. I have here what I call a nature table. These are some of the things I think are beautiful, interesting, and wonderful. I want to share these with you. Gather around the table. Look, even touch and smell if you wish. (In conversation call their attention to the various items, sharing why you think the items are beautiful. Some may think your choices are ugly. You have the opportunity to share more concerning that item.)

4. Of the things on the table, which one thing do you like the most? Can you tell me why? (Again this may be a difficult question for younger children.)

5. God has made a beautiful world. In our prayers let's thank God for the world. Let's each tell each other a short prayer, and each of you thank God for one thing you think is beautiful. I will start. (Give the children a "formula" to follow: "God, we thank you for_____." Give other assistance where needed.)

6. Did you notice the big bouquet of flowers? They are beautiful. I want you to share these with our friends in the congregation. I will give each of you several. As you return to your seats, share them one

by one. Say to our friends, "Here is a flower from God's beautiful world." (Practice the sentence with the children.)

Variations: This event could be used during the various seasons. Objects on the table would reflect the season.

Age suitability: Preschool and elementary.

We Care for the World

Aim: To give the children an experience in caring for the world.

Materials: A bag for each child to be used for collecting trash. Bible (Genesis 1:28). (Have several adults prepared to go outside with the children.)

1. This morning I want to read for you a couple of sentences in the Bible, and I want you to tell me what you think it is telling us. (Read Genesis 1:28. Do not make Adam and Eve the focal point.)

2. There are some big and interesting words in these sentences: subdue, control, etc. (Words will depend upon the translation used.) What do you think these sentences are telling us? (This will be an extremely difficult question for the younger children. They may have difficulty participating verbally. Nevertheless, give them the opportunity. The elementary children will be able to respond more adequately.)

3. I want to share with you what these sentences tell me. God has given us a beautiful world. God wants us to take care of our world and to keep it beautiful. There are many ways that we can help, and I would like for you to help just a little today. Trash makes the world ugly.

4. I have here a bag for each of you and we will do something rather different today. During the sermon I want you to go outside and pick up trash around the church and put it into your bag. Return here soon. After the sermon, you will bring your bag of trash up here. I have asked several adults to go along with you.

5. (After the sermon, ask the children along with the adults to bring the bags of trash to the chancel area.) You have brought back a lot of trash, and I am glad that you helped with the job. When we throw trash on the streets, sidewalks, and the yard, we make the

earth ugly; we do not take care of it. Today, you have helped to remove some of that trash. You have helped to take care of the earth. You have made it a little more beautiful.

6. Let us say a prayer, thanking God for our beautiful world and asking that we learn to care for it and to keep it beautiful. (Compose a short prayer for the children, containing both elements. Practice the words with the children. Pray in unison.)
Age suitability: Kindergarten and early elementary.

We Learn Through Hearing

Aim: To assist the children in recognizing that they learn through the sense of hearing.
Materials: A record or tape containing various sounds; a record or tape player; Bible (Luke 4:42—5:3).

1. (When discussing the senses, remember that someone in the congregation may not have use of one of the senses. Also, the children may know someone who is blind or deaf. Approach such situations in a matter-of-fact manner. Example: "Yes, some people are blind. They must use things other than their eyes in seeing. They use their fingers to read braille. They use seeing-eye dogs.")
2. There are many ways that we learn about our world and life. Can you think of some ways by which we learn of the world? (This can be a difficult question for younger children. For them the world is "just there." Give opportunity for responses. Listen for responses that identify the senses. If a child mentions "hearing," remember that for later reference.) You have made some good suggestions.
3. How do you usually know when it is thundering? How do you know a dog is barking? How do you know when the organ is playing? (Give opportunity for responses.) That's right; we hear those things. Remember, some of you suggested earlier that we learn by hearing. We hear our parents calling, teachers talking, airplanes overhead, fire engines, and many more things. Our hearing helps us to know and learn many things.
4. I have a record (or tape) which has on it a number of sounds. I

will play some, and you try to tell me what they are. (Play several of the sounds, and invite the children to identify.)

5. In the church we learn of God and Jesus; we learn of God and Jesus as we listen and hear. Hearing the sermon and hearing the Bible read are just two ways that we learn and know God and Jesus. I want to read for you just a small portion of the Bible. (Read Luke 4:42—5:3.) What did this short story tell you about Jesus? What are some things he did? (Give opportunity for response.)

6. You can also help people learn and know God as you speak to them words that they hear. As you return to your seats, please stop with several of our friends. Speak a sentence to them: "You belong to God; God cares about you." (Practice the sentence with the children.) *Variation:* Rather than each child stopping with individuals, the children may become a "voice choir" and speak the message as a group.

Age suitability: Preschool and early elementary.

We Learn Through Seeing

Aim: To assist the children in recognizing that they learn through the sense of seeing.

Materials: A small table with three objects of various sizes which are covered; pictures with a Christian motif.

1. (If you are using the series of strategies on the senses, simply refer to what has been discussed previously and begin with #2.) There are many ways that we learn of our world. Can you tell me some of the ways by which we learn? (Give opportunity for responses.) You have made some very fine suggestions.

2. How do you know if the picture is on the television? (One child might respond, "Because you can hear it." You can answer, "You can hear the sound, but can you hear a picture with your ears?") How do I know that your eyes are blue and yours are brown? (A young child might respond, "Because they are.")

3. The table here has several objects on it. (Have the objects covered.) Can you guess what's under the cover? (The forms created by the different-sized objects may give clues for the children's

guessing. If a child does identify one correctly, ask, "What causes you to say that?" Focus on the ability to make appropriate identification by looking at shapes.) Why is it so hard to tell what's there? Yes, they are covered; you cannot see them. So let's take the cover off. Now you can tell for you can see them. (In this strategy do not permit the children to feel the objects. You may need to acknowledge that we might be able to tell if we touched the objects, but the objects will not be touched today.)

4. When we see a thing, it tells us stories about itself. It tells us stories of things and persons. Many of the things that we see in our church tell us stories, especially of God and Jesus. (Point to the various symbols, pictures, and windows in the church. Select several and tell their stories in one or two brief sentences.)

5. I have some pictures which tell us a story as we look at them. (The pictures may be of the church building, copies of a famous painting, a more abstract picture, or several different pictures. Give each child a picture.) I want to share with you the story that I see as I look at the picture. (Again, one or two brief sentences will be sufficient.)

6. You are to keep that picture for yourself. But I have some more pictures here, enough to share with some of our friends here today. I will give each of you some. As you return to your seats, give these pictures to persons in the congregation. You will help them share the story of the picture that they see.

Age suitability: Preschool and early elementary.

We Learn Through Smelling

Aim: To assist the children in recognizing that they learn through the sense of smell.

Materials: Several items of distinctive smells, each in plastic containers; incense; a bunch of flowers; a burning candle.

1. (If you are using the series of strategies on the senses, simply refer to what has been done previously and begin with #2.) There are many ways that we learn of our world. Can you tell me some of the

ways we learn? (Give opportunity for responses.) You have made some fine suggestions.

2. How many of you know what a skunk is? How can you tell if a skunk is nearby even if you cannot see it? Right! Smell it. How many of you have smelled a skunk? Did you like that smell? (Give just a brief time for responses to the questions. You might use another example which may be more familiar to the children, such as a nearby factory.) For each of us there are some smells we do not like.

3. There are many smells that we do like. What are some of your favorite smells? What do you like to smell? (Give opportunity for responses. Some children may still want to talk of smells they do not like—fish, garbage, or even a person. Accept the information but continue with favorite smells.) Smells tell us many things. I know sometimes what I am going to eat for supper just by smelling what's cooking in the kitchen.

4. I have an object in each of these bags. I wonder if you can know what's in each bag by smelling. Close your eyes, and I will let you smell. Don't tell until everyone has had the opportunity to smell. (Pause after the children have smelled one of the objects.) Now, can you tell me what's in the bag? That's right. (Repeat the same process with each object.) Our smelling tells us what is in the bag. (A child may tell you that she cannot smell when she has a cold.)

5. In church there are some smells with which we are familiar. They remind us that we are in church. Can you think of any smells here in the church? (Give opportunity for responses. Most of the children may not be able to respond at all. But some may suggest perfume or candles burning or flowers on Easter Sunday.) In some churches, incense is burned. At one time, many people thought that the smell of the incense was pleasing to God. So they began the practice of burning incense. I have some incense here. Let's burn some and smell it.

6. The flowers in the sanctuary frequently have very pleasant smells. Some flowers have stronger smells than others. Come here and smell the flowers. (Give each child opportunity to smell.) Also, I have another bouquet of flowers. Smell these. Our smelling helps us to learn about our world; smelling helps us to enjoy our world. As you return to your seats I want you to give flowers to some of our friends in the congregation. Say to them, "Enjoy the smell of God's wonderful

world." (Practice the sentence with the children. Give each child several flowers.)

Variation: Rather than the incense (or along with the use of it) you might use candles. Do they ever smell the candles? Do candles ever have a different smell when they have just been put out? Put out a burning candle so that the children may experience a different smell.

Age suitability: Preschool and elementary.

We Learn Through Touching

Aim: To assist the children in recognizing that they learn through the sense of touch.

Materials: Small table with several objects which are covered; a Bible in braille.

1. (If you are using the series of strategies on the senses, simply refer to what has been done previously and begin with #2.) There are many ways that we learn of our world. Can you tell me some of the ways that we learn? (Give opportunity for responses.) You have made some fine suggestions.

2. How do you know if something is hard or soft, rough or smooth, hot or cold, wet or dry? (Give opportunity for responses. Some may say, "Look at it." "Yes, that is possible sometimes, but what if you were blindfolded?") Yes, you touch it; you feel it. We recognize and know a lot about things by touching them, by feeling them.

3. On the table here are some objects which are covered. Rather than seeing them, what is another way of knowing what is on the table? Yes, by feeling them. I want you to put your hands under the cover and let your touch tell you what is there. (The objects should be familiar to the children and not too small or similar.) Don't tell me what is there until all have had a turn. Now that you have all had a turn, what's there? Yes, our touch told us.

4. Some people are blind, and they learn to read with their fingers. I have a Bible here that is written in braille. Words are made by raised dots. (Let the children examine a page, running their fingers over the braille.) Can you read that? Some people are able to read the braille as

they touch the dots and learn to tell the different arrangements of the dots.

5. There are many objects here in our church. I wonder how many of you have touched them. So let's go on a touching tour. (Guide the children, encouraging them to touch the altar or communion table, pulpit, banners or hangings, your vestments, offering plates, carvings, or statues, etc. Simply name the objects. On the tour they may be attracted by something that they have never noticed before and may have a question. Respond simply and directly.)

6. Now you have touched some things in the church. Do you have some favorite things that you like to touch? (You may need to give some suggestions: a stuffed toy, a cat or a dog, soft carpet, a beard, water, etc.) There are some things that I like to touch. (Give an example or two.)

7. Sometimes we touch each other as we meet each other. Can you recall some of those ways? (You may need to give suggestions: handshake, hug, kiss, slap on the back, slapping of palms, etc.) When we do this, we are telling another person, "I am glad to see you; I like you." I am sure that all of you like to get a big hug from Mother or Dad. As you return to your seats, stop with one or two people. Give them a hug or shake their hands. Tell them, "I am glad to see you. First, let me give you a hug." (Hug each child and say, "I am glad to see you today." You might lead the children into the congregation and demonstrate.)

Variation: "How many of you have ever heard of a pet rock? Some people do have a pet rock, a rock that they have found on a vacation or that a special friend has given them. They like to touch and feel the rock. When a friend gives us a rock we might call it a friendship rock. As we feel the rock, it reminds us of our friend. Today I want to give each of you a small rock—a friendship rock—for you are my friends. But I have some more rocks. I want each of you to give a rock to one of our friends in the congregation. As they feel and touch their rocks they will remember our time together today."

(*Materials:* small rocks.)

Age suitability: Preschool and elementary.

We Learn Through Tasting

Aim: To assist the children in recognizing that they learn through the sense of taste.

Materials: Salt, sugar, one or two foods cut into bite sizes. (The food should be covered.)

1. (If you are using the series of strategies on the senses, simply refer to what has been done previously, and begin with #2.) There are many ways that we learn of our world. Can you tell me some of the ways that we learn? (Give opportunity for responses.) You have made some fine suggestions.

2. How do you know if a food is sweet or bitter, salty, peppery, or sour? (Give opportunity for responses.) If you were blindfolded and someone gave you an ice cream cone, how would you know if it was chocolate or vanilla? Yes, you would know by tasting it. If you were blindfolded and someone gave you a piece of fruit, how would you know if it was an apple or a banana? (A child may respond that he could smell it or that the banana would be mushy in his mouth. Recognize that smell and feel are ways of knowing, but ask for another way.) Yes, by tasting we learn something of our foods and drinks.

3. All of us have tastes that we like very much. (You might indicate some of the tastes that you like.) What are some of the tastes that you like? (Give opportunity for the children to respond. Let them vocally agree or disagree with each other. What one child likes, another child may dislike greatly.) Yes, we all have our favorite tastes, but we do differ in our likes, and that's fine. (If children have not indicated tastes they dislike, give an opportunity for that.)

4. I have two small containers. In one is salt; in the other, sugar. Can you tell me which is sugar and which is salt by just looking at them? What would be the best way to know? Taste! All right, take just a bit of each on your finger and taste. Don't tell me which is salt or sugar until all have tasted. (Give each child the opportunity to taste.) Now, which is the salt?

5. I have several pieces of food on the table under the cover. I want you to shut your eyes and taste the food. See if you can tell their

names. (Give each child a small bite of the food.) What did you have? How do you know that?

6. We have been talking about ways that we learn of our world—hearing, seeing, touching, smelling, and tasting. These are our senses. God has made our bodies in wonderful ways and he has given us our senses so that we might learn of the world and enjoy it. So, let us pray and thank God. (You might do the prayer alone or give some help to the children as they compose their prayers.)

Variation: If a congregation practices an early reception of holy communion, the elements used in the sacrament could be used. (If "early" communion is not practiced, we should not use the elements of that sacrament. To permit them to taste the elements while not admitting them to the sacrament of holy communion highlights a particular exclusion.)

Age suitability: Preschool and elementary.

We Say Good-bye

Aim: To enable the children to speak a word of love and to ask God to bless a friend.

Material: None. (To be used when a child is moving from the area. Arrangements should be made with the child's parents.)

1. Have any of you moved from some other city or town to our community here? (Some of the children may remember family moves and may want to tell of the place from which they moved.) Do any of you remember how you felt when you and your family moved from your other house to the one you live in now? Can you tell us about how you felt? (Give opportunity for responses. Many children may not remember a family move.)

2. Let me tell you about how I felt one time when I moved from one place to another. (Share one of your own experiences. Indicate that you were both sad and happy: sad to be leaving good friends, but happy that they were friends and that there were many good times. Indicate that you were not sure what your new community would be like and that you may have been a little frightened. Also, indicate that in your new community you made new friends.)

3. Have any of your friends ever moved away from here to another community? (Let the children speak about their friends.) Do you remember how you felt when your friend moved? (Give opportunity for responses. Many children may not remember the move of a friend and family.)

4. Very soon one of our friends will be leaving, moving to a new community. _____ (*address the child*), can you tell us to where you will be moving? Can you tell us anything about the community? (Give the child an opportunity to respond.) _____, we are sorry that you will be leaving our family here at _____, but we are happy that you have been a part of our family. You will always be our friend.

5. Let's all shake hands with _____, telling _____, "We are happy that you are our friend."

6. Let's ask the other members of _____'s family to come here with us, so that we can all say good-bye to them and we can pray that God will bless the family as they move. (Help the children develop a short prayer and join them in unison in the prayer.)

Variation:

a) When you leave one congregation to assume another pastorate, a similar event can be used. Indicate to the children that you are glad that they are your friends, that you have enjoyed being with them but the time of moving is at hand. Indicate that you will remember them and always be their friend. Shake hands or embrace each child. Close with an appropriate prayer.

b) The strategy could be implemented with those persons who are leaving, even if there are no children in the family.

c) All members of the congregation could be involved.

Age suitability: Preschool and elementary.

Selected Bibliography

Attfield, David G. "Conceptual Research in Religious Education." *Learning for Living* 15 (1976): pp. 91-95.

Batson, C. Daniel. "Creative Religious Growth and Pre-formal Religious Education." *Religious Education* 69 (1974): pp. 302-315.

Brown, George, Jr. "Making Room for Children." *Religious Education* 68 (1973): pp. 401-406.

Cully, Iris V. "The Church's Worship as Formative of the Christian Community." In *Does the Church Know How to Teach?* edited by Kendig Brubaker Cully. New York: Macmillan, 1970.

Durka, Gloria, and Smith, Joanmarie. *Modeling God: Religious Education for Tomorrow*. New York: Paulist Press, 1976.

Fowler, James W. "Stages in Faith: The Structural-Developmental Approach." In *Values and Moral Development*, edited by Thomas C. Hennessy. New York: Paulist Press, 1976.

Furth, Hans G. *Piaget and Knowledge*. Englewood Cliffs, NJ: Prentice-Hall, 1968.

Gobbel, A. Roger, and Gobbel, Gertrude G. "Children and Worship." *Religious Education* 74 (1979): pp. 571-582.

Goldman, Ronald. *Readiness for Religion*. New York: Seabury Press, 1970.

————. *Religious Thinking from Childhood to Adolescence*. New York: Seabury Press, 1968.

Koppe, William A. *How Persons Grow in Christian Community*. Philadelphia: Fortress Press, 1973.

Madge, Violet. *Children in Search of Meaning*. New York: Morehouse-Barlow, 1966.

Maynard, Fredelle B. *Guiding Your Child to a More Creative Life*. Garden City, NY: Doubleday, 1973.

Piaget, Jean. *To Understand Is to Invent*. New York: Penguin Books, 1976.

Riccards, Michael P. "The Structure of Religious Development." *Lumen Vitae* 33 (1978): pp. 97-123.

Sloyan, Virginia. *Signs, Songs and Stories*. Washington: The Liturgical Conference, 1974.

Sloyan, Virginia, and Huck, Gabe, eds. *Children's Liturgies*. Washington: The Liturgical Conference, 1970.

Tarasar, Constance J. "Liturgical Education for Community Life." *Religious Education* 69 (1974): pp. 243-246.

Tobey, Kathrene M. *Learning and Teaching Through the Senses*. Philadelphia: Westminster Press, 1970.

Westerhoff, John H., III. "The Liturgical Imperative of Religion." In *The Religious Education We Need*, edited by James M. Lee, pp. 75-94. Mishawaka, IN: Religious Education Press, 1977.

———. *Values for Tomorrow's Children*. Philadelphia: Pilgrim Press, 1970.

Westerhoff, John H., III, and Neville, Gwen K. *Learning Through Liturgy*. New York: Seabury Press, 1978.